Poetic II *Scripture*

1 Samuel to 2 Kings Stories of the Bible in Poetic Form

LaMar Smith

WESTBOW
PRESS®
A DIVISION OF THOMAS NELSON
& ZONDERVAN

WestBow Press books may be ordered through booksellers or by contacting:

WestBow Press
A Division of Thomas Nelson & Zondervan
1663 Liberty Drive
Bloomington, IN 47403
www.westbowpress.com
844-714-3454

Scripture taken from the King James Version of the Bible.

ISBN: 978-1-6642-6979-8 (sc)
ISBN: 978-1-6642-6980-4 (e)

Print information available on the last page.

WestBow Press rev. date: 07/23/2022

Contents

2 Samuel

Satan/Devil

1 Kings

Inspirational 2

2 Kings

Ladies Chapter

Thank You

What a day to give praise,

Because the Lord has awoken me today.

Now I am thanking Him for His love,

Thankful for the one true God above.

Thankful for the air I breathe,

And for loving me when I didn't believe.

Thank you for the food I eat,

And yet some starve for days and weeks.

Thank you that I'm able to give to those in need,

Thank you that I'm able to comfort those who grieve.

Thank you for the water I'm able to drink,

Thank you for my mind and I'm able to think.

Thank you for my job, which is a blessing,

Now I'm on bended knee and I'm confessing.

I thank you for sparing my life,

And watching over this sinner every night.

Thank you for fighting my battles hidden from my sight,

I am grateful none can withstand your power and might.

I am thankful for your grace and mercy,

And that I'm not alone, you are walking with me.

I do not need to walk through the valley of death,

Nor do I need to be close to my last breath.

I am thanking you now and every day,

I thank you more and more as I pray.

I can thank you during the good times,

I know you have never left my heart and mind.

Thank you for watching over me,

Thank you for putting your spirit in me.

Thank you for all my family and friends,

We pray together and know that this is not the end.

Thankful that you will come again in your Father's name,

Thankful I'm able to stand for you unashamed.

With your bloodshed on the cross,

I'm thankful all is not lost.

Thankful for the lamb's blood of your son,

And I know the darkness will never come.

With all the struggles in my life,

Thankful for Jesus because He is the light.

No matter how depressed or feeling down,

The first shall be last and the last will wear a crown.

Thankful for the power in Jesus' name,

Thankful He can break every chain.

I am thankful for my redeemer,

I am thankful for my deliverer.

I am thankful for my provider,

I am thankful for my healer.

Thankful no weapon forged against me will prevail,

This is your promise Father, and you never fail.

The mountains may shake, and the hills may be moved,

Thankful for your unfailing love that can never be removed.

Thankful for the first day you breathed life into me,

You have blessed me with your grace and mercy.

Thankful for being slow to anger and abounding love,

Thankful for the one true God above.

Thankful for my guardian Angel as my protection,

And for listening to my prayers as our connection.

Thank you, Father you are my everything,

Thanking you when I lift my voice and sing.

Father, I can go on and on,

This would be an endless poem.

All you have done and all you will do,

I will end this by saying, I love you.

Amen

Special Thanks

Always, first, I thank the Heavenly Father for His blessings, grace and mercy. It is a joy having the Father giving me another opportunity to write another book in His honor. I truly hope you enjoyed Poetic Scripture Genesis to Ruth stories of the Bible in poetic form, my first book. We will continue with 1 Samuel and end with 2 Kings, again lifting the Heavenly Father's name in honor with poetry. He deserves so much more than I can give. He has given me so much mercy and grace and I know I do not deserve it. I have been forgiven, my life saved and showered with blessings.

I hope you have your bibles with you as most of the poetry in this book is scriptural based. As a reference, I used the King James Version but please use the version you are most comfortable using. We should take delight in the reading of His words. The only way, I think, is to have a version that keeps you engaged, not confused. Just as the first Poetic Scripture book, this is another useful tool to use to spread the words of the Father. As we grow as a person and with God, what we read when we were younger, may have a different meaning today. Therefore, I believe, each time we read the Bible it is like an entirely new book. God is amazing. Keep praising His name and continue praying for each other.

I must give praises and love to my wife Melody Smith and my mother Yvonne Smith; may she rest in peace. A true warrior for God. She has taught me so much and my beautiful wife keeps me grounded. The words are difficult to express the love I have for them both, but I attempt to honor them in poetry. Mom I love you and Melody, you have my heart.

I thank my brothers and sisters that corrected me when I was wrong and placed me back on the path: Ronn L. Davids and Monica L. Davids, Teddy T. Taylor, Becky Sharpe, Jennifer D. Roan and Aunt April Hardnett. Thank you to the pastors spreading the word of God.

Introduction

Again, this is a poetic style summation of stories in the bible, giving a different style reaching an audience enjoying God's words. The questions at the end of most poems will make you think about your own life as it relates to the story in the bible. This is not a replacement of His words, only a different avenue with poetry that leads you back to His word. Please enjoy and pray for me as I pray for you. We all need to sincerely pray for each other and to lift one another up in times of need. Always have your favorite bible with you as we take this journey together.

1 Samuel

The book of 1 Samuel is the start of the Israelites having a mortal king rule over them and the consistent rejection of the Lord. This is also the journey of a man after God's own heart, David. Saul is Israel's first king as requested by the Israelites. We also read about Eli and his sons' errant behavior in the decline of the priesthood. Saul's relentless pursuit of David as jealousy rules his heart and his refusal to go to God first. As we read and study, because I know you got your bibles with you, we will learn, grow, and love the Father's words. The theme has not changed from the first Poetic Scripture book Genesis to Ruth; please have a translation you understand and enjoy reading. Remember four pages per day and you can read the bible in one year.

Given to the Lord

Hannah prayed for a son,

She was downhearted because she had none.

Year after year, they would go to Shiloh to worship and sacrifice,

And every year, Peninnah would ridicule Hannah out of spite.

Elkanah would give Hannah one choice portion of meat,

He asked, "Why are you crying, why don't you eat?

Don't be downhearted because you do not have my seed,

It is better than ten sons because you have me."

Once in Shiloh, after a sacrificial meal,

Hannah prayed to God, and she made a deal.

She vowed to God," Look upon me, my prayer and give a son to me,

I will give him to You for his entire lifetime is my decree."

Eli the priest saw her lips moving but not a sound,

He asked, "Must you come here drunk on sacred ground?"

"No sir, I am praying with a heavy heart and in distress,"

Eli said, "In that case, go in peace and may God grant your request."

They returned home and God remembered her prayer,

He gave Hannah a son and her heart no longer despaired.

"When Samuel is weaned, he is with the Lord permanently,"

"Stay here and may God help you keep your promise", Elkanah agreed.

After Samuel was weaned, they took him to Eli the priest,

Hannah asked, "I am the woman praying, do you remember me?

I asked for a son,

Because I had none.

The lord granted my request,

Now I do what is best.

My heart rejoices in the Lord,

There is none holy like the Lord."

This was Hannah's prayer,

When her heart was in despair.

Please read all of Hannah's prayer in chapter two. It is powerful and moving as she gives honor and praise to the Most High. Who thinks prayer doesn't work? How many times have we read about the power of prayer? How much power is in a mother's prayer? I know my mother prayed over me to keep me safe and healthy. How many of us pray over our children? We must come to God with an honest heart and soul when we pray. Keep in mind, God will hold you to your promise.

When Eli saw her lips moving, he assumed that she did this before in the past or did he react too quickly? She made a deal with God, and He will always claim His debt one way or the other. Please be very careful when you pray and make promises to the Father. In this instance, all worked out for the best. Have you ever made a deal with God? If so, have you paid your debt to Him?

(1 Sam 1:3-7, 1 Sam 1:8, 1 Sam 1:9-17, 1 Sam 1:19-28)

Spare The Rod

When the people offered sacrifice, it was practiced by the priest,
A servant will come with a fork and get a share of the meat.
Whatever the fork brought up while the meat was being boiled,
Eli's sons were scoundrels and God's Holy sacrifice was soiled.
All the Israelites that came to Shiloh, this is how they were treated,
Even before the fat was burned, here comes the servant of the priest.
"Hand the meat over or I'll take it against your will,"
Soon the Lord knew, Eli's sons, He would have to kill.
Sleeping with the women at the entrance of the tent of meeting,
Eli said, "Your wicked deeds, why do you do such things?
If one sins against another, God may mediate,
But sinning against God, what is their fate?"
Their father's words, Eli's sons did not hear,
No love for God nor did they have any fear.
God said, "Under Pharaoh, did I not clearly reveal myself to their family?
I chose your ancestor out of all the tribes to be my priest.
My share of My sacrifice goes to your son's mouth,
Why do you scorn My offering I have for My house?
Therefore, the Lord, the God of Israel now declare,
Your family would minister before me, now beware."
One day, a man of God came to Eli the priest,
And told him how God will cut off his family tree.
"I choose your ancestor Aaron from among all the tribes,
To wear the vest, burn incense and offer sacrifice.
You and your sons have taken the best offerings and become fat,
You give Me no honor and your faith continue to lack.
I promised your branch of Levi would always be my priest,
I will despise dishonorably those who think lightly of me.
The time has come your family will no longer serve as my priest,
They will die before their time as they watch Israel's prosperity.
No member of your family will ever live out their days,
Survivors will live in sadness and grief will be their way.

And their children will die a violent and horrible death,
Hophni and Phinehas on the same day will take their last breath.
Then your surviving family will beg for food and money,
They will say please give us jobs so we will have food to eat.
Then I will raise up a faithful priest, serving Me in many things,
I will establish his family to be My priest and to anoint kings."

How long did it take your parents to discipline you for your bad behavior? Why did Eli not call his sons out on their behavior? After all, wasn't he the head priest? What's the old saying again, spare the rod and spoil the child? How true. Was he more focused on doing God's work? Can we be so Heavenly minded that we are no earthly good? We should have a balance of life, God, and family. But, as we read further, the Father of us all, called all three of them out on their behavior. Eli for his lack of discipline and his two sons for their wickedness. Do we sometimes think that because our parents have not said anything, it means they do not know? Be mindful of your actions, especially while doing work in the name of the Lord! I am sure He knows and sees all.

(I Sam 2:12-16, I Sam 2:22-29, I Sam 2:30-36)

Failed Restraint

Again, Israel and the Philistines are engaged in mortal combat,
The Philistines killed about 4,000 Israelites during their attack.
The elders of Israel asked the returning soldiers *why*?
"Now let's bring the Ark, so that it may save our lives."
The elders were very puzzled why they were defeated,
Believing the Ark would save them from their enemies.
The people sent men to Shiloh to bring back the Ark,
Eli's two sons, Hophni and Phinehas also arrived with the Ark.
With great joy, the Israelites shouted as the Ark is in their hands,
The noise shook the grounds where the Philistines stand.
The Philistines asked," What is this noise reaching our ears?"
When they learned the Ark had come, the Philistines had much fear.
"We are doomed, the gods that killed the Egyptians with their might,
Be strong, do you want to be slaves? Prepare yourselves to fight."
And fought they did, 30,000 Israelites soldiers were laid to waste,
The Ark of God was captured, and Eli's two sons went to their graves.
Later, a Benjamite from battle went to Shiloh with dust on his head,
How can he tell the town the Ark is gone, and Eli's sons are dead?
Eli in his chair on the road, for the Ark of God, his heart had fear,
The man entered the town, told the news and they cried out in tears.
Eli was old, whose eyes failed so that he could not see,
Eli was told, "Your sons are dead, and the armies' losses are heavy.
Israel's army fled, and the Philistines, the Ark, they did take,"
Mentioning the Ark, Eli fell off his chair by the side of the gate.
He broke his neck,
Only his daughter-in-law was left.
The wife of Phinehas went into labor when she heard the news,
Gave birth to a son, but by the labor pains she was subdued.
The woman attending her said, "Don't despair, you have a son,"
But she didn't pay any attention, nor did she respond.
She named him Ichabod, saying, "For the Ark of God is taken,
The glory has departed from Israel, it is forsaken."

I must take you back to 1 Sam 3:11-14. The words God swore by, about Eli's sons. Again, God keeps his promise. Should Eli have disciplined or restrained his sons for or from their sins? Do you discipline your children? Did the Israelites put the Ark ahead of God? It seems as they came close to idol worshipping the Ark. If they came to God first, would they have lost? Relying more on a symbol of former victories and turning away from God. More lessons that keep repeating itself. Place God first and go to Him first. How can you go wrong? Now I know you have your bibles with you in a translation that you understand. Keep reading and keep enjoying His words.

I have also lived in the past of what God has done for me instead of looking at the here and now. In my mind, He always takes care of me, instead of keeping my relationship new and fresh. I needed to pray and understand a spiritual victory comes from continual prayer and faith in God.

(1 Sam 4:1-4, 1 Sam 4:5-10, 1 Sam 4:12-15, 1 Sam 4:17-21)

Dagon's Temple

The Philistines took the Ark from Ebenezer to Ashdod,
They placed it in Dagon's temple and set it beside Dagon, their God.
And when the people of Ashdod rose early the next day,
Before the Ark of God, Dagon had fallen on its face.
They took Dagon and put him back in his place,
But the next morning, Dagon had fallen exactly the same way.
This time, what was broken off were his head and his hands,
Ashdod people said, "The Ark of the Lord can't stay in these lands".
The Lord's hands were heavy on the people of Ashdod and its vicinity,
He brought devastation on them with tumors; His hands were heavy.
Ashdod asked the rulers, "What can be done with God's wrath?"
The rulers said, "Have the Ark moved to the city of Gath."
The Lord's hands weren't any lighter because of what they had done,
He caused great destruction in Gath sending the Ark to Ekron.
The people of Ekron thought the Ark was sent to lay them to waste,
Crying out to the Philistines rulers to send it back to its own place.
After seven months, the Philistines called for the priests,
"Tell us how to send the Ark back, so that we may have peace".
They said, "Send it back with a guilt offering as a gift,
Then you will be healed, and the Lord's hands will lift.
Send back five golden emerods and five gold mice,
This way the Lord will remove the tumors and strife.
Why do you harden your hearts as the Egyptians and Pharaoh?
God dealt with them harshly and they let His people go.
Now with two cows, have calved and never been yoked to this day,
Hitch the cows to the cart but take the calves and pen them away.
Put the Ark and offering on it and watch where it goes,
Depending on which way, this is how you will know.
If it goes to its territory, then God has taken a stance,
If it does not, then we know our disaster happened by chance."
The cows went to Bethshemesh, the territory of its own lands,
The Philistines knew this was the work of God's own hands.

The people of Bethshemesh were overjoyed when they saw the Ark,
They sacrificed the cows and for fire, they chopped up the cart.
Some being overcome with joy, inside of the Ark they looked,
God struck them down, in all, over 50,000 lives He took.
"Who can stand before God, where will the Ark go from here?"
Kirjathjearim men took the Ark, it stayed there for twenty years.

God did say He was a jealous God. Need I say more? The Ark was in the house of Abinadab, 1 Sam 7:1. Do false Gods have the same power as the one true God? Do some research and find out about Dagon, Judges 16:23. Do we worship items in place of God, even if it has a symbolic meaning? Do we need a picture of the cross just to know God is present? Alternatively, a picture of Jesus? Whether we have a cross around our necks or pictures all over our houses, do we need that to have faith? Perhaps, a good reminder but that's all.

A powerful story when you think about it. For a cow to pass by its nursing calf, it is going against all its motherly instincts. I believe this was done to show all who have the power, which is God. He sent the cow to Israel showing He has power over the natural order of life and death. God is not just an ingredient to a great life, but He is the only ingredient of life.

(1 Sam 5: 1-6, 1 Sam 5:7-12, 1 Sam 6:1-4, 1 Sam 6:6-9, 1 Sam 6:13-21, 1 Sam 7:1-2, 1 Chron 10:8-10)

The Eye of Nahash

Saul went back to Gibeah to his home,

A group of scoundrels complained, making him king is wrong.

They scorned him and their hearts had dissention,

But Saul ignored them, he paid no attention.

During this time, Jabeshgilead was seized by the Ammonites,

The men of Jabesh were afraid and didn't want to fight.

The people of Jabesh asked for peace,

"We will be your servants," they pleaded.

Nahash said, "I will gouge out the right eye of all to disgrace Israel,

This is the only way my hunger will be fulfilled."

Elders saying, "Let us send messengers to Israel, give us seven days,

If no one comes to save us, we agree, and will become your slaves."

Saul had been plowing the fields when the messengers arrived,

The people broke out into tears hearing the gouging of eyes.

Saul asked, "Why are you crying, what is wrong?"

After he heard the news, the Spirit of God came upon him strong.

The oxen he had been plowing the field with, he cut them into parts,

With a strong message, hoping it would light a spark.

"Refusing to follow us into war, this is what your oxen will look like,"

Terror fell on the people; they came out as one, ready to fight.

Over 300,000 men ready for battle, ready to jump in the fray,

Saul sent back messengers, and this is what they had to say.

"By noon tomorrow, you will be rescued, you will be free,"

Saul mobilized them at Bezek, a strong and powerful army.

There was great joy when the messengers arrived,

Knowing that Nahash would not gouge out their eyes.

Jabesh said, "Tomorrow we surrender, do as you please,"

Later Saul arrived and in three divisions, he divided his armies.

With the three detachments, he slaughtered them all morning long,

No two Ammonites together escaped to their homes.

Then the people wanted to kill those opposing Saul's rule,

They exclaimed, "We will kill them before we are through."

But Saul replied, "No one will be executed today,
The Lord has rescued Israel and lighted their way."
Then Saul said, "Let's go to Gilgal and have offerings."
In a solemn ceremony before the Lord, they made Saul king.

Wow, how cruel to gouge out people's eyes! We may not go to this extreme, but do we harm others spirits or feelings just to make a point? I think the term now is bullying. There are many forms of being a bully: physical, mentally, social media, words, and other forms. Remember the phrase, an eye for an eye? If this is true, the problem is, it will leave everyone blind. Leave the final justice to the Father. Allow Him to fight your battles for you. I am sure He is undefeated.

As a leader, everyone criticized Saul; it comes with the position. Saul didn't pay any attention to the critics this time but would be consumed with jealousy later 1 Sam 19:1-3. As a leader, you should listen to constructive criticism but not waste time or energy on those who oppose you by reacting. Ask God how you can channel your anger and emotions into positive attributes. Saul became king even though Samuel warned Israel about having a human king 1 Sam 8:10-18.

(1 Sam 10:26-27, 1 Sam 11:1-3, 1 Sam 11:6-11, 1 Sam 11:12-14)

Obedience Over Sacrifice

For two years as king was Saul's reign,

God has rejected him, and only Saul is to blame.

From the army's special troop, Saul selected 3,000 men,

1000 went with Jonathan to Gibeah in the land of Benjamin.

At Geba, the Philistine garrison was defeated by Jonathan,

Saul blew the ram's horn, and the Israelite army was summoned.

The Philistines' army of 30,000 chariots and 6,000 charioteers,

The men of Israel saw this massive army and they trembled in fear.

Hard pressed by the enemy, they hid in rocks, thickets, and caves,

Saul realized that his troops were rapidly slipping away.

Saul was at Gilgal waiting for Samuel for seven days,

As instructed by Samuel until he arrived at him during the day.

Impatient, Saul demanded, "Bring me the peace and burnt offering!"

But then, Samuel arrived just as Saul was finishing.

Saul went to meet him, and Samuel asked, "What have you done?

This is not the instructions given to you by the One."

Saul replied, "You didn't arrive on time and my men are rattled,

And the Philistines are at Michmash and ready for battle.

I haven't asked the Lord, so I felt compelled to do it myself,"

Samuel exclaimed, "How foolish not to ask the Lord for help!

Forever your kingdom would be if you kept His command,

Now it must end, for the Lord has sought out another man.

One who is after His own heart,

One that will keep His command from the start."

Saul continued his reign as king,

Continued to realize what disobedience brings.

"Go and destroy the nation of Amalek completely,

Men, women, cattle, goats, sheep, children and babies."

One day, Samuel said to Saul, "This is the message God shares,

This is His message of settling accounts He has declared."

At Telaim, Saul mobilized the entire army,

They went to a town and lay in wait in the valley.

Saul sent a warning to the Kenites,

"Move away or you'll be destroyed in the fight.

You showed kindness when we came out of Egypt,"

Therefore, the Kenites packed up everything and left.

From Havilah to Shur, they slaughtered the Amalekites,

They destroyed all but spared King Agag's life.

The Israelites kept the best sheep, goats, cattle, and lambs,

Once again, this wasn't a part of the Lord's command.

God said to Samuel, "*It repenteth me that I ever made him king,*

He has not been loyal, refused to obey and dishonored the offerings."

Samuel was deeply moved,

However, the Lord's words he did not refuse.

The next morning, Samuel went to Carmel, one of the towns,

Moreover, Samuel could not believe what he had found.

Saul set up a monument to himself,

Disobeyed God and kept the Amalekites wealth.

Saul greeted Samuel, "God bless you, I have obeyed His command,"

Samuel said, "If this is true, why are cattle spread over the land?"

"It's true, the army spared the best for sacrifice," Saul said,

Samuel said, "The Lord said, destroy all, He wanted everything dead.

Why did you rush to plunder and do evil in the Lord's sight?

So, let me tell you what the Lord said to me last night.

Obedience and submission are better than sacrifice and offering,

You rejected the Lord's command; He has rejected you as king!"

I am sorry I ever made him king. What a statement from the Lord. This poem is two chapters, but both reflect Saul's disobedience to God. Do as He commands because God knows what is best for us. Only a little patience would have saved Saul's kingdom. Is this not true today? We must have it now and not have any patience to allow God to do what's best. Would there be a David if Saul was obedient? Are you being obedient to God's commands? Another question, are you listening when He calls? What good are sacrifices if we fail to obey?

Luke 13:18-19 is a great reference that can be applied towards patience. Faith of a mustard seed, and when it grows, it becomes a tree with branches. You have to water, fertilize and care for the entire process for it to grow. Is it any different with your patience in the process of your faith?

(1 Sam 13:1-4, 1 Sam 13:5-13, 1 Sam 15:1-6, 1 Sam 15:5-10, 1 Sam 15:12-15, 1 Sam 15:17-26)

Quiet Honey

Now the Israelites were in distress this day,

This is what Saul had to say.

"You are bound under oath before me,

A curse to anyone before this evening who eats."

The army entered the woods and they saw honey oozing out,

No one touched it; no one put his hand to his mouth.

None except Jonathan,

This is Saul's son.

He dipped his staff, tasted the honey and it brightened his eyes,

"Your father bound us under oath," stated a soldier by his side.

"Curse anyone who eats today, that is why we are faint and weak,"

"My father had made trouble; my eyes brightened after the honey.

If the men had eaten, how much better would it be?

Slaughtering the Philistines and taking plunder from our enemies."

They struck down the Philistines, butchered cattle and ate,

Saul looked at them and said, "You have broken faith,

You are eating meat with blood still inside."

Saul built an altar because he tried to do what was right.

Then Saul said. "Let's pursue the Philistines and leave none alive,"

"Do whatever seems best to you," the army replied.

But the priest said, "Let us inquire here to what God has to say,"

Then Saul asked God, but God was silent that day.

Therefore, Saul said, "Let's find out where the guilt lies,

Even if the guilty is Jonathan, then he must die."

Saul prayed to the Lord to seek out the guilty party,

"Cast the lot between my son and me."

The guilty was found to be Jonathan his son,

Saul said, "Tell me what you have done?"

"I tasted honey with the end of my staff, now I must die,"

Saul said, "May God deal with me if I don't do what's right."

But the men said," Do not harm a hair on your son,

He brought Israel deliverance, he's the reason we won."

Saul stopped the pursuit and his army he withdrew,
Saul is king over Israel; it is his rule.

Is this a situation when we should make inquiries before pronouncing sentences? In other words, innocent until the facts have been produced. Or is ignorance of the law no excuse? 1 Samuel 8:10-18 the Israelites were warned what a king would do. Keep reading about Saul because his journey takes a turn for the worse. I know your Bibles are right by your side and you are reading four pages per day. God is good!

How faithful was Jonathan! He was ready to die, and he spoke the truth of his error. This also shows the great respect the men had for Jonathan. They defended him at his time of need. Do you speak up when you are wrong? Do you blame others? We should always speak the truth and own up to our wrongdoings. What is the point of lying? Eventually the truth will come out and God knows all anyway.

(1 Sam 14:24-28, 1 Sam 14:29-36, 1 Sam 14:41-47)

Not by the Cover

The Lord said to Samuel, "*Your mourning for Saul has been long,*
Go to Bethlehem and find Jesse, one of his sons to me belongs."
But Samuel said, "If Saul hears about it, he will kill me,"
God said, "*Take a heifer as a sacrifice and invite Jesse.*"
Samuel arrived in Bethlehem and the elders trembled in fear,
"What's wrong? Do you come in peace, why are you here?"
Samuel said, "Purify yourselves and come with me to the sacrifice,"
Samuel purified Jesses and his sons that night.
Samuel looked at Eliab and thought, this is the Lord's anointed,
God said, "*Not by appearance, I will tell you who is appointed.*"
One by one,
Came all of Jesse's sons.
None was chosen from the start,
Because the Lord looked into their heart.
Samuel asked, "Are these all the sons you have?"
"There is still the youngest", Jesse replied, "He is the last."
They would not eat until David arrived,
He was dark and handsome with beautiful eyes.
And the Lord said, "*Anoint him, he is the one,*"
And the spirit of the Lord was with him from that day on.

How about the old phrase, don't judge a book by its cover? Samuel probably thought because Saul was tall, Eliab would be God's choice. As the Lord explained, I see more than just the outward appearance. I see the heart. Do we judge just by the external features? How many times have you taken the time to explore further than the surface? Do you only see a person by their attractive looks? A cute smile? What they wear? Take time to find out if they are just as attractive inside, you might be surprised with the answers you find.

I am guilty of the same. In my younger days, the cover was all I needed when searching for a date. I think, sometimes, it is human nature. However, as we grow and mature the same cover may not be as attractive as it once was. Remember the same can be true when others are looking at your cover.

(1 Sam 16:1-13)

Harder They Fall

Goliath stood and shouted a taunt across to the Israelites,

"Why are you all coming out here to fight?

I defy the armies of Israel today,

If your champion kills me, then we'll be your slaves."

Over nine feet tall and with his armor, Goliath was a sight,

Just standing there had Israel armies in fear and fright.

His armor was bronze, and he carried a spear like a javelin,

A spear with an iron spearhead and an attitude that he will win.

His armor bearer walked ahead him carrying a heavy shield,

His armor and weapons were impossible for one man to wield.

But there he stood taunting all of Israel's armies,

For forty days, daring anyone to come out and fight me.

Saul had offered as a reward, no taxes, and his daughter as a wife,

If anyone challenges the Philistine's champion and takes his life.

David checking on his brothers heard the taunts of the giant man,

Saying, "Who is this Philistine pagan that no one will take a stand?"

David's brother Eliab said, "I know about your pride and deceit,

Why are you here, shouldn't you be watching after those few sheep?"

Soon, others David began questioning,

After a while, David was sent for by Saul the king.

David said to Saul, "Don't worry; I'll go out to fight,"

Saul said, "You are only a boy, he'll take your life."

David persisted and Saul gave him his armor to wear,

David said, "I didn't have these for the lion or the bear."

Five smooth stones in his bag, David started across the valley,

Goliath walked out saying, "Am I a dog that you should face me.

Coming with staves, I'll give your flesh to the birds." Goliath said,

David said, "Today God will conquer you and I'll take thine head."

As Goliath moved in for the kill,

David was doing the Lord's will.

With sling and stone, David hit his mark,

David, God's choice, a man after His own heart.

Goliath stumbled and fell in the presence of the Lord,

David ran over and killed Goliath with his own sword.

David removed it from its sheath and cut off his head,

The Philistines watching turned and ran, seeing Goliath dead.

Next, David returned to Saul with Goliath's head still in his hand,

And King Saul was curious, asking, "Who is this young man?"

Did Goliath size make him a bully? He was 6 cubits and a span, which makes him over nine feet tall. He carried over a hundred pounds of armor. This was a mountain of a man! Sometimes the loudest one in the room is the least to act. Confidence versus arrogance is a fine line. Which one are you? When you have an undefeated record, the only place to go is down or to lose, unless you are God. When you are fighting for the Lord, does it matter how big and ruthless your adversary is? All you need is faith and believing the Lord will fight for you.

Goliath was a bully and his great size made him justify his actions. When people are in terror at the mere sight of you, it probably gives you an ego. Never be afraid of anyone as long as you trust God and have true faith. One question, what can't God do?

David had a different perspective of Goliath. All David saw was a large target to hit, defying the almighty God. No matter the criticisms or negative comments, David was determined to face down the Giant. When you do what is right and pleasing to God, opinions do not matter. It will not be the last time Goliath's family faces David and the Israelite army, 2 Samuel 21:19. When faithful, God will give you a different point of view when confronting "Giant" problems. All are small problems when you turn them over to God.

(1 Sam 17:4-8, 1 Sam 17:16, 1 Sam 17:25-29, 1 Sam 17:32-45, 1 Sam 17:36, 1 Sam 17:48-50, 1 Sam 17:55-57)

In-Laws

On Saul, God placed a tormenting spirit,

David played a harp that gave Saul a good lift.

Whenever Saul was with fear and depressed in his heart,

David would come and send the spirit away playing his harp.

David became Saul's armor bearer in service to the throne,

Saul was so pleased; he didn't want David to go home.

Later, David slew Goliath and became commander over the men,

And this is when David and Jonathan became friends.

Jonathan sealed the pact by giving David his robe,

Together with his tunic, sword, belt, and his bow.

David was always victorious,

This made Saul furious.

The women would come out from the towns,

Joyous, with tambourines and cymbals, singing and dancing around.

Saul has killed his thousands,

And David has killed ten thousand.

Saul said, "Next they will make him king,"

Jealousy has a way of twisting some things.

Saul was overwhelmed by the tormenting spirit the next day,

Like a lunatic in his house, Saul began to rant and rave.

In his rage, he tried to take David's life,

He threw his spear, but David eluded him twice.

Saul being afraid of David, he sent him away,

But David continued to love Saul and served with faith.

David did everything with great success,

Passing yet another one of Saul's tests.

Saul's eldest daughter was David's reward,

Saul thought the Philistines would put David to the sword.

"Who am I to become the king's son-in-law?" David said,

Merab, Saul's daughter, was given to Adriel the Meholathite instead.

A second chance to become his son-in-law by daughter number two,

Saul said, "You can marry Michal, but this is what you do.

The price for the bride is one hundred Philistine's foreskins,"
This was Saul's wicked plan to have his revenge.
He thought Michal and the Philistines would put David in a trap,
David went out with his men and brought 200 foreskins back.
Saul realized the Lord was with him,
Saul became afraid of him.
Saul remained David's enemy the rest of his days,
God continued to bless David with mercy and grace.

Again, an evil spirit in 1 Samuel 16:14 reference, read about the evil spirit. Was the spirit called jealousy? When David became king, he sent one of his men on an impossible task to die 2 Samuel 11:14-15, only he succeeded in 2 Samuel 11:24. Did Saul see his kingdom slipping away? When you observe someone at your job doing a better job than you do, do you get angry? Do you call them names? Remember verse six, all the women came out and sang about David. As a king, Saul was furious, not all the attention was on him.

If we put all that God has given us to the job He has given, jealousy would never happen. God places you in a position for a reason, do your best until He moves you. Doing half the job deserves half the reward. My philosophy has always been that work integrity can't go wrong.

(1 Sam 18:1-8, 1 Sam 18:10-14, 1 Sam 18:18-21, 1 Sam 18:24-30, 1 Sam 16:14-15)

Naked Prophet

Saul told his son Jonathan and all present, he wanted David dead,
"My father Saul is looking for a chance to kill you," Jonathan said.
"Tomorrow be on your guard and go and find a place to hide,
Until I speak with my father and then come to your side."
Jonathan told David this because they were friends,
Jonathan and David made a pact until their life's end.
Jonathan said to Saul, "Let not the king raise his hand,
To do harm against David, an innocent man.
He has not wronged you and his deeds benefit you greatly,
He slew the giant Goliath and for all of Israel; a great victory."
Jonathan stated facts and, in his heart, he has hope,
Saul listened to his son, and then stated this oath.
"As surely as the Lord lives, David will not be put to death,"
Jonathan was relieved his friend would not take his last breath.
David once again was with Saul and everyone was at ease,
But how long could it last, how long will there be peace?
Soon again, with the Philistines there were hostilities,
David struck them with such force, the Philistines had to flee.
While in his house, God sent an evil spirit on Saul,
He threw a spear at David and drove it into the wall.
This is not the first time Saul did this in his sickened state,
Late that night, David knew he had to leave and escape.
Saul sent men to David's house to stalk and kill his prey,
Michal said, "If you don't run tonight, you'll be slayed."
Later, Michal let David down a window, and he fled,
She took an idol, covered it, and placed goat's hair at the head.
When the men entered, Michal said, "He is unwell,"
All they found was an idol in the bed, Saul's plan failed.
Saul was unsettled but he knew he had David on the run,
David escaped; he went to Ramah and told Samuel what was done.
In Naioth, David and Samuel decided to stay,
Word came to Saul and he sent men to capture him that day.

But when they got there, here is what they saw with their eyes,

Samuel standing as leader with a group of prophets prophesying.

The spirit of the Lord came on them and they prophesied,

Saul sent more men and they too prophesied.

Saul sent men a third time and the results were the same,

No one can resist the awesome power of the Lord's name.

Finally, he, himself went to Ramah; he needed to be a witness,

But alas, even a king can't escape the Lord's Spirit.

He stripped off his garments and prophesied in Samuel's presence,

Laying naked all day they asked, "Is Saul among the prophets?"

Hatred, vengeance, and jealousy are very powerful emotions. However, the name of the Lord has much more power. So much so, it had Saul naked and prophesying. Can you imagine that? What kind of actions blind raw emotions have you been doing? Hopefully, not wanting to kill someone. Nevertheless, how far did you go? We should not let these types of emotions get the better of us. There is a better way. Sometimes we need to take a time out and step away from the situation to get a better understanding. In addition, it never hurts to get advice from the Most High first before acting.

A true testament of friendship, Proverbs 18:24. So much so that Jonathan told David his father's plan instead of acting on them. Can you go against your family even if they are wrong? As a person of faith, you should be able to call anyone out if they are in the wrong. Sometimes, it is how you tell them they are wrong can make all the difference in the world.

(1 Sam 19:1-6, 1 Sam 19:8-14, 1 Sam 19:18-23)

Edomite the Priest Killer

With spear in hand, in Ramah, under a tree,

Saul asked his officials, "Have you all conspired against me?

Why has no one told me my son made a pact with the son of Jesse?

And that he lies in wait, none of you are concerned about me."

Doeg spoke, "David came to Ahimelech and inquired of the Lord,

He gave David provisions and Goliath Philistine's sword."

David must move from place to place,

But Saul was in pursuit and not given up on the chase.

Now the king sent for the priest Ahimelech and all his family,

Asking the same question, "Why have you conspired against me?

He has rebelled and lies in wait for me as he does today,

You gave him supplies and a sword, what do you have to say?"

Ahimelech answered, "None is more loyal than your son-in-law?

It was not the first time I inquired for him; did I break any law?

Is making accusations against your servant, is the way of the king?

For your servant isn't aware of this affair, I know nothing."

The king said, "Ahimelech you and your entire family will perish,"

Saul ordered the guards, "Take out your swords and handle this!

They have sided with David; turn and kill the priests,

They knew he was fleeing, yet they did not tell me."

The officials were unwilling to strike down the priests of the Lord,

The king ordered Doeg, "Kill them, put them to the sword."

He struck them down, the Edomite,

That day he took eighty-five men's lives.

Doeg also put to the sword, Nob, the town of the priests,

Men, women, children, infants, cattle and sheep.

But Abiathar escaped to David, he managed to flee,

David said," Don't be afraid, you will be safe with me."

If Saul was king, why was he so focused on David? Now Saul refused to trust those most close to him including his son, daughter, priest, and his loyal men. We should never let rage take over so much that it blinds us to the truth. Reason and rational thinking are no longer in the mind. When emotions are this high, this is the time we need to ask the Father for strength and answers to our problems. Saul failed to seek God and listened to someone not Godly. In the heat of things, sometimes there is always someone pushing you to the edge of acting and later having enormous regret.

Remember the Israelites asked for a king. This shows how a man can become an evil tyrant. God does not promise evil will not be in this world but does promise those who are faithful will experience great rewards. There may be a time you come face to face with evil, are you ready? Do you have all that you need to battle evil? Ephesians 6:11-18

(1 Sam 21:7-9, 1 Sam 22:6-8, 1 Sam 22:11-14, 1 Sam 22:16-18, 1 Sam 22:20-23)

Corner Robe

After pursuing the Philistines, these are the words to Saul's ears,
"By the Rocks of the Wild Goats, David and his men are near."
Saul took 3,000 from all of Israel able young men,
A cave was there when he came along to the sheep's pens.
Saul went to relieve himself inside of the cave,
Not knowing, David and his men could make it his grave.
The men said, "I will give your enemy to do what you wish,"
David cut a corner piece of Saul's robe going unnoticed.
David was conscience stricken,
Thinking to himself, this is wicked.
He said to his men, "He is anointed by the Lord,
I can't put my master to death with my sword."
Saul left the cave and went on his way,
Stopping suddenly with the words David had to say.
"My lord the king," David said with his face to the ground,
This is the sight Saul saw as he turned around.
David said, "Some urged me to kill you,
But my lord I have spared you.
This day you have seen with your own eyes,
The lord delivered you and I didn't take your life.
Look at the corner of your robe in my hand,
There is nothing to indicate that I am an evil man.
From evil doers come evil deeds,
May the Lord judge between you and me.
Against whom do you pursue, a dead dog, after a flea?
The Lord therefore be the judge and deliver me."
Saul asked, "Is that your voice David my son?"
This is what Saul said after David was done.
"You are more righteous than I," he said,
"You have treated me well and I could be dead.
And I have treated you badly,
Listening to all the good you did to me.

Unharmed, does an enemy let him get away?
May the Lord reward you well with your treatment today.
I know that you will surely be king,
Now swear to me not to kill off my offspring."
To Saul, David gave his oath,
Saul left, and David went to his stronghold.

What would you have done? Would you have struck him down knowing he is the Lord's anointed? Would your conscience have gotten to you as much as David's? A tough decision to wipe out your enemy now or let them live to rise again. As we keep reading, Saul's pursuit is far from over. This is just another reason why God chose David because He looked into his heart. Remember obedience over sacrifice will take you a long way. Perhaps all the way to the throne. Keep reading with a bible translation you understand and enjoy.

We can also see the respect David had for Saul and the position Saul held. Sometimes we lose sight of the position a person has by only evaluating the person and bringing those emotions inward. What kind of precedent would David make by assassinating the King? We should respect elected officials and persons in authority. Romans 13:1-3 teaches us about governing authorities.

(1 Sam 24:1-4, 1 Sam 24:5-13, 1 Sam 24:16-22)

Soft Touch of a Wife

At Carmel a man in Maon had property,

He had goats and sheep; he was very wealthy.

He was Nabal and Abigail was his wife's name,

A churlish man that was mean and surly with no shame.

David was in the wilderness, he heard Nabal was shearing sheep,

He sent ten men to Nabal, "And in my name, you should greet.

Wish him and his household good health and long life,

While your shepherds were with us, they suffered no strife.

As your own servants, we didn't mistreat them the entire time,

Therefore, be favorable with your servant David whatever you find."

David's men delivered the messages and waited for a reply,

Nabal answered with disrespect and with much despise.

"Who is David, who is the son of Jesse, who is he?

Why should I take bread, water and give him meat?

Many servants are breaking from their masters these days,"

David's men turned around and repeated every word Nabal did say.

"Each of you strap on your sword," David said to his men,

About four hundred went with David to teach Nabal a lesson.

One of the servants told Abigail about the meeting,

Saying Nabal spoke insults instead of warm greetings.

"The entire time we were around them, we were treated fair,

If nothing is done about these insults, I feel a sense of despair."

Abigail acted quickly,

She knew it would get messy.

She took bread, wine, sheep, figs and loaded her donkeys,

She loaded other items with her servants very silently.

Abigail didn't tell her husband because he was a wicked man,

She hurried to David because she knew he would raise his hand.

She sent her servants ahead before she left the scene,

As she came riding her donkey into a mountain ravine.

There was David and his men,

Armed and ready for the battle to begin.

27

David saying, "He paid me back evil for good, it's been useless,
Watching over this fellow's property and this is his gift."
Seeing David coming; she got off her donkey and bowed at his feet,
"Pardon your servant my lord and let me speak.
He is just like his name, his name means fool,
I know the Lord is with you and He wants you to rule.
Your enemies He will sling out as the middle of a sling,
Your life will be bound securely in the bundle of the living.
He has kept you from vengeance and bloodshed off your hands,
You fight the Lord's battles because you are a righteous man.
And when the Lord your God gives you success, remember me."
David said, "Praise to the Lord for bringing you for me to meet.
If you did not come, all males would be dead by daybreak,
I accept your gifts; go in peace for Nabal's sake."
Abigail returned to Nabal and he was having a feast fit for a king,
She waited to tell him so he could understand everything.
He was sober now and Abigail told him of the tale,
He became like a stone, in his chest his heart just failed.
Nabal died in about ten days,
David heard of this and the Lord he praised.

Abigail's touch of a wife provided the needed time for God to get involved. Romans 12:19 speaks on vengeance. Her quick thinking looking at the bigger picture, promoting peace between the two men, saved lives. We should look beyond the narrow crisis at hand and realize there is something bigger to focus on. She was in a difficult position, between a husband and a future king not in a mood to listen.

Have you ever been in a situation or saw one where it seems a conversation is about to escalate into an all-out war? I have. Both sides refuse to back down and neither wants to. Just when the situation is about to go to the extreme, a woman walks in and cools down both sides. Most of the time she is the mother, grandmother, or wife, gives a look, points a finger, or tells a funny story and both sides start to laugh or cool off. A soft, but stern touch of a woman can ease most situations if the correct words are expressed.

How much time does it take to listen to the other side before acting? I think it's not very long, but I am guilty of reacting first. Are you? The bigger picture of reacting hastily is cleaning up the mess afterwards. You may have apologies to make, mend broken friendships and reconciliation with family. Sounds exhausting and very time consuming, versus a few minutes it takes to listen. Ask God for patience, guidance and wisdom and you can't go wrong.

(1 Sam 25:2-7, 1 Sam 25:10-13, 1 Sam 25:18-28, 1 Sam 25:32-35, 1 Sam 25:36-38)

The Spirit of Samuel

When Saul saw the Philistine's army, he inquired of the Lord,

He got nothing from dreams, Urim or prophets, he was ignored.

All familiar spirits and wizards were expelled from the land,

It was Saul's own fault, done by his order and his own two hands.

Saul had so much fear in his heart,

Ordering, "Find me a medium before war starts."

They said, "There is one in Endor nearby,"

Saul put on other clothes in disguise.

Saul went to the woman and said, "Bring forth the one I name,"

She said, "Surely you know Saul's order, this is a dangerous game.

This is a trap, I can't do this,

He cut off all wizards and familiar spirits."

Saul swore to the Lord, "You will not be punished for this,"

She said, "Who shall I bring up, I will do what you wish."

"Bring me up Samuel," he said,

She brought up Samuel from the dead.

Upon seeing him she said, "You are Saul, why did you deceive me?"

Saul said, "Don't be afraid, tell me what you see."

"I see a ghostly figure approaching,

From the Earth an old man with a robe coming."

Then Saul knew it was Samuel and he bowed down,

Prostrated himself with his face to the ground.

Samuel said, "Why have you disturbed me by bringing me up?"

"I am in great distress," Saul said, "And I am stuck.

God has departed from me and I don't know what to do,

No dreams, no prophets; therefore, I have called on you."

Samuel said, "Now God has departed, and He is your enemy,

The Lord almighty has done what He predicted through me.

The kingdom is out of your hands and into another,

Tomorrow you will join me with your son and his brothers.

Because you failed God's wrath against the Amalekites,

Israel's army will fail against the Philistines, no matter their fight."

Immediately Saul fell full length when the words reached his ears,

His strength was gone; he was hungry and a heart full of fear.

The woman and his men urged Saul to eat,

She butchered a calf and made bread without yeast.

She said, "Your servant obeyed you, my promise I kept,"

She gave them food and that same night they got up and left.

Saul had to desperately seek advice from the same things he banned. He publicly removed this type of sin from the land but not from his heart. He denounced sin but still committed sin. If Saul had listened to God, God would have answered his prayers. Don't be surprised if God does not answer you when you have disobeyed Him. Like the very old saying, desperate times call for desperate measures.

Keep in mind when the medium saw Samuel, she knew right away, it was Samuel and not a false image. Did God allow this to deliver His message directly to Saul? We always need to remember God will use whom He wants to deliver His message. Remember Balaam in the book of Numbers?

(1 Sam 28:3-7, 1 Sam 28:8-13, 1 Sam 28:15-19, 1 Sam 28:20-24)

Inspirational 1

I Love You

There is nothing I wouldn't do for you,

Remember that I love you because I created you.

When you didn't believe and lost your faith,

Think of what I did and think of what I gave.

I gave you my only begotten son,

While you were sinning and having fun.

As a parent, you should know your child's worth,

I made him mortal and placed him on this Earth.

Is there anyone here today?

Whether you have faith or lost your way.

Believes I will not do all that we may become one,

I will forgive and show mercy so you can get to my Kingdom.

This is how much I love you,

This is what I will do.

From the first time I breathed life into you,

I knew then that I love you.

From the time you ate the fruit from the tree,

And the serpent lied, and you were deceived.

From the time Noah built the Ark,

And I sent the great flood grieving my heart.

Remember, no matter what you do,

My love is unconditional for all of you.

Even when you cursed my name,

And when you didn't stand because you were ashamed.

No matter how much you have sinned,

Remember, a sin is a sin.

As Christians, are you on your high horse?

It's about my word, so please stay the course.

The course is that I love you all,

I am here to pick you up when you fall.

My word says, come as you are,

Even if you strayed off the path too far.

If you want to be a self-righteous man,
I can write all your sins in the sand.
Don't ever forget the mission,
To become a better Christian.
To bring all people to me,
No matter what are their belief.
All the time your faith goes through a test,
Hold steadfast and you will be blessed.

Street Walker

I have walked these streets for so long, I think I'm lost,

I have to find him no matter what is the cost.

I asked for directions, for someone to show me the way,

I couldn't get an honest answer, no one gave it to me straight.

I just walked three blocks on Forgiveness Lane,

It was full of mirrors and I had only myself to blame.

The next block was full of friends and family,

But also full of fingers pointing back at me.

I just kept walking until I came to block three,

It was a dark block, full of nothing but enemies.

Then I made a right on Perseverance Street,

By the time I got off, my back hurt and pains in my feet.

Now, all this walking has taken a heavy toll,

I think I'm lost again; I came to a fork in the road.

Should I go left on Hope or a right on Faith?

Both have heavy traffic no matter which one I take.

It was just my luck, a man stood with a smile on his face,

He said, "No matter which path, they both end in the same place."

I took a right on Faith and couldn't even see the end,

I shook his hand and said, "I'll take Hope next time my friend."

Will I make it to my destination, will I reach my spot?

Word on the streets says the block is hot.

I wish it were a shortcut,

And I hope I don't get stuck.

But like it says, enjoy the journey,

Soon your eyes will open and see.

After time, I didn't pay attention to street signs,

After the right on Faith, now I'm walking blind.

As soon as I look up, I'm at the corner of Grace and Mercy,

And there is my destination, waiting for me.

And He says, "I have more blessings to give,

You are the reason why I have lived.

I know your journey was long and full of sorrow,
But always remember, I will be here tomorrow.
If you have any doubt,
I never run out.
I was with you and kept you safe,
I was there when you walked on Faith.
Three blocks on Forgiveness Lane, I was with thee,
And kept you close on Perseverance Street.
Remember each fork in the road leads to me,
No matter what, I always have what you need."

Gifts

1 Peter 4:10

Dear Father,

Please allow me to use all my gifts,

You give me,

To serve others and glorify you.

By serving others,

I serve you.

Let me serve with honor,

With humility,

With dignity,

By your grace.

As you command.

With a cheerful heart.

Amen.

Spin It

Once again, spin negativity,
Into positivity.
No matter the pandemic,
No matter the epidemic,
God is here,
God is near.
The Devil is in your ear,
With faith, have no fear.
I have been close to death,
Family members have taken their last breath.
Sometimes, I don't have food to eat,
Today, I don't know how ends will meet.
Rent and mortgage is due,
Baby crying and there's no food.
I go to the mailbox and there's only bills,
I got a bottle of alcohol and a handful of pills.
I'm at my end with an eyeful of grief,
I cry out and drop to my knees.
I take responsibility for my part,
Psalms 31:24, I will be of courage and shall strengthen my heart.
The only way to spin it, is to serve,
Luke 4:8, thou shalt worship the Lord and only Him shall you serve.
I have only one way for the answers I seek,
Is to open my mind and heart and let Jesus speak.
Is there anything God can't do?
This is the question I have for you.
If you take the truth and not believe the lies,
The Father will always be by your side.
In closing, you shall know this,
Titus 1:2 God will always fulfill His promise.

Amen.

Broken

I stand before the Father, what do I bring?

I have no sacrifice; I have no offering.

Will I stand with an attitude?

Or will I stand in gratitude?

The books are open of all my sins,

The Angel reads them off and there seems to be no end.

I stand accused,

Ignorance of the law is no excuse.

I am guilty,

Father, please forgive me.

I come to say that I am broken,

I come to confess all my sins.

There are no sins that I am exempt,

Because for all of them I had contempt.

Please hear my confessions as I repent,

During years of sinning, my life spent.

I can tell you where I went wrong,

Because my sins have lasted for so long.

You know of my deceitful ways,

Because every day I went astray.

I am so broken,

Now I want to come in.

I have broken too many laws,

Father, I know I am flawed.

I am here at your feet,

Twisted, broken and full of deceit.

How can I pass through the pearly gates?

While on this Earth still having hate.

I want to walk on the golden streets,

But evil in my heart still has a beat.

I took your name in vain,

Even I was ashamed.

You knew me before I was conceived,

You knew what I thought and what I believed.

Now I am nothing at your feet,

Asking for forgiveness, please.

This is where I come off my sinful road,

This is where I come to save my soul.

Please look at my spirit,

I hope you will cherish it.

Only you have the power to say yes,

Only you can say I am blessed.

Only you can call me home,

Only you can reserve a seat by your throne.

Asking for forgiveness with a bowed face,

The forgiveness of sins, according to the richness of his grace.

Ephesians 1:7

Amen.

Home with the King

God called my name that only I could hear,

And at that moment, the Angels drew near.

He has called me home,

I'm with the Father at his throne.

Remember me as I lived,

Remember all the love I had to give.

I am never really gone,

Because to all of you I belong.

I am always close and always near,

Listen to your heart and you will hear,

The Ram's horn sounding for so long,

Heaven's Angels are singing me a song.

While all of Heaven is celebrating only for me,

This is why all of you must hold on to our family.

I am home with the Father and Son,

In all of you, my memory will live on.

No matter where you are,

No matter how close or how far,

Remember I was always a fighter,

In all of you, our family will shine brighter.

Do not stand at my grave and weep,

I will be at the Pearly gates when we meet.

Family and friends, lift your voice and sing,

I am no longer with you, but I am home with the King.

Not those 3 Letters

Three letters with enormous power.

I am sorry…but,

I apologize…but,

I would have done this…but,

I would not have said this…but,

I was going to help…but,

I see you on the side of the road…but,

What if Jesus used this powerful word?

And for the sake of this piece, I'm going to add some extra.

I was going to listen to your prayer…but,

Too many voices that I couldn't hear yours.

I was going to feed you…but,

I only had a couple of fish.

I was going to heal you…but,

I'm not a doctor.

I was going to die for your sins…but,

You constantly disrespect me.

I was going to forgive you…but,

You killed me.

How would you feel if Jesus were to use these three letters when we needed him the most? But….

Cooking with Soul

A pinch of mercy,

A dash of grace,

Add a pound of praise,

Slowly pour in humility,

Stir in a stick of salvation,

Constantly add forgiveness,

Sprinkle in some worship,

Tablespoon of patience,

Cup of guidance,

One jar of wisdom,

A few leaves of hallelujah,

Whip with the spoon of blessings,

Let it sit in your heart,

Pour in a bowl of love,

Serving size – All.

2 Samuel

This is the story of David as king, his struggles as a man and
his downfall. David proves to be more human than most.
Born halfway between Abraham and Jesus, David
stands out as a godly role model more than most
in the bible. Even a man after God's own heart fell
to sin and forgiveness through repentance. David's
story could not have been written in today's world
by any writer in modern history as a classic novel
than this. David's story has romance, love, war, death,
friendship and betrayal; what more could a novel give to
us? As you read God's words, you find so much positivity
from these same circumstances as they occur.

Saul's death vibrates through Israel and David. David could have
killed Saul on more than one occasion but refused to lay hands on
God's anointed, fearing God's wrath. David becomes King but
his reign is full of rebellion from his own family, as you will
read by his own actions. We also learn in this book, the birth
of King Solomon, the builder of God's temple and a man of
great wisdom. I know you have your favorite Bible with you as
you read four pages per day in our goal to read the Word in a
year. Please enjoy.

News Ill Received

A man arrived with his clothes torn and dust on his head,

Informing David, the king and his sons are dead.

He paid David honor by falling face first to the ground,

"I have escaped the Israelites camp and I am no longer bound."

David asked, "What happened, what has occurred?"

He told David everything, these are his words.

"The men fled from battle," he replied,

"Saul and his sons are no longer alive."

David said, "How do you know this?"

He replied, "I was there, I was a witness.

I was on Mount Gilboa and there was Saul leaning on his spear,

And in hot pursuit was a group of charioteers.

He saw me and called out; I said what could I do?

Then he asked; who are you?

An Amalekite, I replied,

Anguish is upon me but I'm still alive.

Stand here by me and kill me,

This is what Saul said to me.

Then I stood beside him and put him to the sword,

Took his crown and bracelet and brought them here to my lord."

David and his men tore their clothes because of the news received,

They fasted until evening, they mourned, and they grieved.

David asked, "Weren't you afraid to kill the anointed of the Lord?"

Then David called one of his men to put the man to the sword.

"Your blood be on your own head,

Your mouth testified against you by what you said."

Being the bearer of bad news seemingly was not a good job. This person was more than likely a scavenger seeking a reward because the account of Saul's death was entirely different from this man 1 Samuel 31:3-4. Being a liar only brought him disaster and his life ended. David had just destroyed a band of Amalekite raiders 1 Samuel 30:17 and he probably wasn't aware of this fact and chose to act as a friend of Israel. A lesson of lying and deceit never pays off.

Proverbs 12:22 and Proverbs 19:9. How much did David have to endure to become king? How much could you endure to accomplish a goal?

David had to overlook offenses by Saul and others to survive and await God's promise. How much patience do you have when others cause you embarrassment or harm? We need to practice patience with all situations in our lives with empathy and forgiveness. The quick reaction, most times, is not the best method to guide us. A quick prayer for patience, guidance and wisdom will lead to the best solution to any scenario. Please read David's song to Jonathan and Saul as a tribute to his friend and former king.

(2 Sam 1:1-4, 2 Sam 1:6-12, 2 Sam 1:19-27, 1 Chron 10:4-6, 1 Chron 10:8-10)

Gazelle's Spear

Both sides of Israel met at Gibeon's pool,

Twelve men from both sides chose to have a duel.

Twelve from David's and twelve from Saul's,

Ready to fight in a free for all.

All twenty-four men died,

Grabbing each other's hair and thrusting their sword in the side.

Abner was defeated by David's men that day,

But in the fierce battle a huge price was paid.

Abner looked back and said, "Asahel, is that you?

Go and chase someone else, I don't want to kill you.

Get away, if I kill you, how could I face your brother?

Take on one of the younger men, go and chase another."

Asahel refused, he was hot on the trail,

Pursuing Abner relentlessly, he could run like a gazelle.

Because Asahel refused to stop his attack,

Abner thrust the butt of his spear through his rib and out his back.

Joab and Abishai pursued Abner until sunset,

To avenge their brother's death without regret.

Atop of a hill Abner's men formed a group,

They were with him; these are his troops.

Abner called out, "How long will you pursue your fellow Israelites?

Must the sword devour forever and take many lives?"

Joab said," Had you not spoke, we would pursue all night,"

Joab blew the trumpet, and all the troops stopped the fight.

The sons of Zeruiah revenge never left their minds,

As you keep reading, you find out it was just a matter of time.

Also, during this time, Abner had his position strengthened,

Ishbosheth was weak and needed to cause some type of dissension.

Stating, "Why did you sleep with my father's concubine?"

Abner responded angrily thinking Ishbosheth had lost his mind.

"Am I a dog's head, I have a great deal of loyalty,

I haven't handed you over to David; this is how you treat me?

Yet now you accuse me of this offense,

May God deal with me if I do not do what's promised.

Give David's throne over Israel and Judah from Beersheba to Dan,"

Ishbosheth didn't speak to Abner because he was afraid of the man.

Abner's story is not over by far,

The brothers seeking revenge still have wounds and scars.

David is now only King over Judah, and the rest of Israel seems to be faithful to Saul. Samuel has already declared David King, but the actual public ceremony has yet to take place. Neither side gained an advantage and the civil war continued. Abner was Saul's commander of the army and pursued David in Saul's quest to end David's life. They both saw each other across the battle lines multiple times.

Abner, a fierce warrior, warned against Asahel chasing after him leading to his death. Persistence is a valuable trait if it is for a worthy cause. However, if the goal is a personal one, then it could be no more than stubbornness. Which are you? A tale of vengeance has just begun with Joab.

(2 Sam 2:12-16, 2 Sam 2:17-23, 2 Sam 2:24-29, 2 Sam 3:6-11, 1 Chron 11:6)

Double Agent

Abner sent messengers saying, "Doesn't the entire land belong to you?
Make a pact with me and I will help turn all Israel over to you."
David said, "Yes but bring me Michal my wife,
That I paid for with one hundred Philistines' lives."
Abner returned with Michal and David was pleased,
So much so, David entertained them with a great feast.
Abner said, "They will make you their king, let me call an assembly,"
David agreed and sent Abner safely away in peace.
Soon after Abner left and Joab arrived,
Still with vengeance in his heart and burning eyes.
Joab rushed to the king and said, "Why did you let him get away?
You know he is here to spy on you, you will be betrayed."
Messengers caught up to Abner and he came back,
David not knowing of Joab's planned attack.
Joab took Abner to the side as if to speak to him privately,
Then stabbed Abner in the stomach, killing him violently.
When David heard of the crime, he made this declaration,
"I and my kingdom are pure; a curse on all of Joab's generations.
May a man have open sores or leprosy,
Walk on crutches, die by the sword or beg for food to eat."
The death of his brother Asahel price is now paid,
David ordered Joab and his men to mourn Abner to the grave.
David refused to eat no matter how much the people begged,
This pleased all knowing Abner's death wasn't on David's head.
"Joab and Abishai are too hard for me, even though I am king,
May the Lord repay these evil men for doing such a thing."

Abner's loyalty switched with whoever was in power or he thought would be victorious.
Abner made the mistake of saying *he* would give the throne to David, but that was God's
promise not Abner's. Do you know anyone like this? Always switching sides or straddling
the fence?

Joab took revenge instead of letting God handle His justice. Considering Joab killed Abner in a city of refuge Joshua 20:1-6, David also disobeyed God's laws. Joab was a mighty warrior and seemed to want his own flexibility not having to answer to anyone. A powerful statement by David in 2 Samuel 3:39, *too hard for me, even as king to control.* We can look at this in a few different ways: friend, warrior, fear, loyalty, or another reason for the lack of discipline. Either way, this is not the last time Joab does what he wants without David disciplining him. David's family becomes more of a thorn than he wants to deal with. Keep reading.

(2 Sam 3:12-21, 2 Sam 3:22-30, 2 Sam 3:31-38, 1 Chron 11:6)

Constant Thorn

Saying to David, "While Saul was king, you led his military,"

They made a covenant and anointed David king at the age of thirty.

Marching to Jerusalem to attack the Jebusites,

"You can't get in here, even the lame and those without sight."

Nonetheless, David captured the Zion fortress,

He built up the area around it inward from the terraces.

In the city of David, a palace for David was built during this time,

Leaving Hebron, David took more wives and many concubines.

More children were born,

But the fighting would go on.

The Philistines in full force went out into the Rephaim lands,

David asked God, "Shall I attack, will you give them unto my hands?"

The Lord said, *"Go it will be done."*

Defeated, but once again did they come.

Once again seeking God's counsel, David asked,

God said, *"Don't go straight up but circled around back,*

As you hear the sound of marching in the tops of the mulberry trees,

Move quickly, the Lord is in front to strike the Philistine army."

Another victory as God has planned it,

All because David did as the Lord commanded it.

How long and how many times did the Israelites have to fight the Philistines? What do you think is the reason for this continuing war between these two nations? The Zion fortress seemed to be impenetrable by the appearance, but when God is on your side, nothing is impossible. Remember Jericho, Joshua chapter 6. As long as we seek God's counsel first, how can you go wrong?

We can spin this to ask, how many times must you face the same temptation? Every time we go left or right, the same temptation is right there. Just as a thorn in our side, the nagging pain or reminder of not going away. Sometimes, the same temptation can come back after years of prayer and adjustments. Nevertheless, there is great news, once you recognize the same temptation but in a different form, you know what it is and just keep moving forward. You have prayed for strength to overcome and to not to be tempted again. God can give you that strength. What an amazing God we serve.

(2 Sam 5:1-4, 2 Sam 5:13-19, 2 Sam 5:22-25, 1 Chron 14:8-17)

The Architect

David was settled in his palace and God has given him rest,
The Lord used the prophet Nathan to deliver His covenant.
The Ark was placed in a tent, which was on David's mind,
Moving it from Jerusalem and to Abinadab's house for some time.
At the threshing floor of Nachon, God's anger, Uzzah's life was paid,
David was angry because of God's anger; he was still afraid.
For months Obededom's house was blessed just as Israel's nation,
David now moved the Ark with sacrifices and great celebrations.
Michal, the daughter of Saul, came out to meet him in disgust,
Seemingly angry and she may have lost all trust.
"The King exposing himself to servant girls shamelessly,"
David said, "Dancing before God who chose me over Saul's family."
David spoke to Nathan about the resting place of the Ark,
The Ark resting in a tent weighed heavy on David's heart.
Nathan said, "Go ahead and do whatever, the Lord is on your side,"
But later the Lord spoke to Nathan that same night.
The Lord said, "*Tell my servant, these are my words I speak,*
The Lord has declared, are you the one to build a house for me?
I have never lived in a house,
From the days of Egypt, I took my people out.
From place to place; a tent, a tabernacle is where I stayed,
No matter where, I have not complained on any day.
Now go and say to David, I took you from tending sheep,
However, you will not be the one to build a house for me.
I will raise up one of your descendants, your own offspring,
I will secure his royal throne forever and produce future kings.
Furthermore, the Lord declares that He will make a house for you,
I will discipline him with the rod, as any father would do.
Unlike Saul, My favor will not be taken,
For all time, your throne will not be forsaken."
Nathan informed David that the Lord said no to his plans,
David was thankful and prayed that he was an unworthy man.

Uzzah was only trying to protect the Ark. But does God really need protecting? A valiant effort but only the Levites were supposed to handle the Ark and it was a capital offense to touch it, Numbers 4:15. Remember, enthusiasm must be accompanied with obedience to his laws.

Why was Michal so angry, or was it jealousy? 2 Samuel 6:20, Then David returned to bless his household. David did not forget to come and bless his family as well as all of Israel but still met with contempt. 2 Samuel 6:23, therefore Michal the daughter of Saul had no children until the day of her death. A feeling of bitterness and resentment that goes unchecked pays a heavy price. We need to check our unfounded resentment and bitterness if we don't want to pay the price of destroying a relationship.

David, being grateful and thankful for all his blessings, gave a prayer of thanks to God. Sometimes when we feel unworthy, it is the time we are most worthy of His blessings. No matter how small a gift given, always give praise to the Father. He woke you up this morning, which is a blessing.

(2 Sam 6:1-10, 2 Sam 6:16-23, 2 Sam 7:1-3, 2 Sam 7:5-8, 2 Sam 7:10-16, 2 Sam 7:17-30, 1 Chron 13:7-10, 1 Chron 17:7-14)

Eyes of an Hawk

David got up and walked around the roof of the palace one evening,

From there he saw a beautiful woman bathing.

He needed to know who this woman was that just entered his life,

He found out she is the daughter of Eliam and Uriah's wife.

Just knowing of her, David was not satisfied,

He sent for her, slept with her and now in her belly a new life.

A prince,

She is pregnant.

Through word by Joab, "Send me Uriah the Hittite,"

Planning a diabolical plot to take his life and steal his wife.

"How are the soldiers and the war going?" David asked Uriah,

Hoping no one would become the wiser.

David said, "Go home and wash your feet,"

However, Uriah slept in the streets.

Later, David asked, "Why did you not go home to your family?"

Uriah said, "How could I when your men are camped in open country?

As surely as you live, I will not do such a thing,

I will not go home, make love to my wife and eating and drinking."

Uriah stayed one more day at David's invitation,

David got him drunk with a celebration.

Uriah did not go home, he slept on his mat amongst the servants,

Now, David really knew his fate and what this truly meant.

The saying, *don't' kill the messenger,* in this case wasn't true,

The letter David gave him for Joab, gave details on what to do.

"Put Uriah where the fighting is the fiercest, and then withdraw,

I am sure he will be struck down and he will fall."

Joab sent message, the battle was fierce but moreover Uriah is dead,

Joab explained so the king's anger wouldn't fall on his head.

To king David the messenger reported back,

David said, "The sword devours one as another, press the attack."

Bathsheba mourned and she was in grief,

With all David did, the Lord was very displeased.

Just as a predator, David watched and captured his prey. In 2 Samuel 11:4, she just finished purification rites, which means she was not already pregnant when David slept with her. How much did David sin during this situation? Lust, deceit, murder, desire and how many more can you name? David failed to run from his desires and temptations. Most of all he failed to speak to the Lord for guidance. Was Bathsheba innocent in all of this? Did she know the king would be walking during this time? And why was she bathing for all to see? Did she tempt the King to sleep with her?

In my younger age, I was equally as guilty to falling to my desires and lust. How about you? Some of us may not admit to them but we all have our failings. God knows. A great lesson about reaching out to God, stopping sin before it starts. You have read how far David plotted to get Bathsheba for himself. Do you think because he was the king, he thought he could do anything? This attitude later in 2 Samuel comes back to confront him in dealings with his sons.

(2 Sam 11:2-5, 2 Sam 11:6-11, 2 Sam 11:12-16, 2 Sam 11:25-27)

The Ewe and the Successor

Nathan was sent to David as God's choice,

To express God's displeasure to be His voice.

David unaware of the events to unfold,

This is the story Nathan told.

"In a certain town, there were two men,

One had an ewe that grew up with his children.

It shared his food, drank from his cup and slept in his arms,

This was all the poor man had and he kept it from harm.

The rich man had a large number of cattle and sheep,"

David listened to Nathan very attentively.

"Now one day a traveler to the rich man's home he came,

Preparing a meal not sacrificing his own sheep, the man refrained.

Instead, he took the poor man's ewe for the mealtime feast,"

David burned with anger in utter disbelief.

David said, "The man who did this must die, he had no pity,"

Nathan said, "The man who did this, is now standing before me.

God says, *I anointed you king over Israel, I gave you all,*

I gave you your master's house and delivered you from Saul.

And if this was too little, I would have given you more,

Why did you despise my word and strike Uriah down with the sword?

You took his wife to be your own,

Now the sword will never depart from your home.

I will bring calamity on you before your very eyes,

Someone close to you, I will give them your wives.

This will be done in broad daylight,

You did your sin in secret under the cover of night.

This will be done before all of Israel,

You have sinned, you have done evil."

David said to Nathan, "Against the Lord I have sinned,"

Nathan replied, "The lord has taken away your sin.

Even though you have sinned, you will not die,

For your utter contempt for God, your son will lose his life."

David pleaded with God for his son, and he fasted,
Within seven days, God's words came to pass.
No one wanted to tell David about his son's death,
But he heard them whispering under their breath.
This is when he knew his son was gone,
David changed his clothes and ate after fasting for so long.
Advisors didn't understand, "You wept, fasted and refused to eat,"
David said, "I shall go to him, but he shall not return to me."
Eventually, David and Bathsheba birthed another son,
The builder of God's house and they named him Solomon.

Whatever is done in the dark will be brought to light. How many of us believe in this statement? What made David think God would not know about his treachery? After all, God was with David in all things. I love how God uses parables to show us our own sins. Even after the story of the ewe, God did punish David by taking their son. Noticed I said *their* son, because was Bathsheba innocent in all of this?

What was Solomon's name the Lord told Nathan to tell them? In 2 Samuel 12:25 the name is Jedidiah which means beloved of the Lord. Do some research, was this the only time the name Jedidiah used in reference to Solomon? Solomon's story will soon be told. Keep reading and keep delighting in the Lord.

(2 Sam 12:1-5, 2 Sam 12:7-11, 2 Sam 12:13-18, 2 Sam 12:20-25)

A Chip Off the Ol Block

Amnon fell in love with Tamar over the course of time,

Being his half-sister, was this love being blind?

Nonetheless, he got advice from a very shrewd man,

His name was Jonadab, his friend, he had advised a plan.

Jonadab said, "Go to bed and make yourself sick,

And when your father comes to see you, here is the rest of my trick.

Tell him you want Tamar to cook and feed you with her hand,"

David said, "Go to your brother and prepare food," was his command.

She took dough, kneaded it but he refused to eat the bread she baked,

Amnon commanded all to remove themselves from his place.

He told Tamar, "Bring the food into this chamber so that I may eat,"

Amnon had another reason; his father and brother will be displeased.

Then he grabbed her and said, "Come to bed with me,"

"No, my brother, don't force me and don't do this to me.

Don't do this wicked thing, where could I get rid of my disgrace?

You would be a wicked fool and where could I show my face?

Please speak to the king,"

The act was done, he wasn't listening.

Amnon was stronger and committed the act of rape,

He said, "Get up and get out," the love quickly changed to hate.

"No," she said, "Sending me away is more wrong and more severe,"

His hatred was so intense all her words never reached his ears.

Calling his servants, "Bolt the door, remove her from my sight,"

How could Amnon think treating his sister this way was right?

Tamar tore her robe, cried and placed ashes on her head,

Now her brother Absalom saw her sobbing, and this is what he said.

"He is your brother, hold your tongue and hold your peace,"

While Absalom's anger swelled, and thoughts of vengeance increased.

It took two long years,

To wipe away Tamar's tears.

Absalom waited two years to come up with a master plot,

Undoubtedly thinking that his father and brother must have forgot.

A short memory of rape,

And a long stay of hate.

Absalom invited the king and all his sons to come and celebrate,

David said, "If we all come, the burden on you will be too great."

Absalom said, "Please send all the kings' sons and my brothers,

It will be a feast for a king, unlike any other."

David gave blessings and soon he agreed,

Absalom prepared his men for the deed.

"When Amnon is drunk, kill him at my command,

Have courage, I gave the order, it is by my hand."

On signal, Amnon was murdered,

All the other sons fled on mules in terror.

The report reached David, all his sons killed, not one is alive,

Just then, Jonadab arrived and said, "No that's a lie.

Absalom has plotted this for two years, now he has escaped and fled,

Ever since Tamar was raped; only Amnon is dead."

David saw all of his sons weeping before his eyes,

Rape and death were the fall of David's kingdom as God prophesied.

I am surprised David failed to discipline his son for raping his virgin daughter. Considering God did speak to him about Him disciplining David's son in the future in, 2 Samuel 7:14. Let's not fail to mention the friend in all of this, it was his scheme. Is it the case of a confidant edging him on to do wrong? Or could it be a case of being and or thinking I'm privileged? Royalty?

Love and lust are two different things. Lust is the here and now and love is patient and takes time to develop. A few scriptures of love taken from 1 Corinthians 13:5 and verse 13. *Doth not behave itself unseemly, seeketh not her own, is not easily provoked, thinketh no evil.* And verse 13, *and now abideth faith, hope, charity, these three: but the greatest of these is charity.* Which truly translates; love is the greatest of all. Amen

(2 Sam 13:1-4, 2 Sam 13:5-10, 2 Sam 13:12-20, 2 Sam 13:23-25, 2 Sam 13:28-39, 1 Cor 13)

Privileged

Absalom was praised to be very handsome and flawless,

Cutting it once a year, his hair was five pounds when he weighed it.

He lived in Jerusalem for two years and never got to see the king,

Punishment for killing his brother Amnon while they were feasting.

Absalom asked Joab to intercede twice, but was refused,

Inside of Absalom's heart, his anger swelled, and it grew.

Absalom told his servants "Set fire to Joab's fields next to mines,

Maybe he will come; maybe this will change his mind."

Joab asked, "Why did your servants set my fields on fire?"

Absalom replied, "Why can't I be placed before the king's eyes?

If he finds me guilty of anything, let him kill me,"

David summoned Absalom, kissed him and they had peace.

Treachery is not far behind,

Absalom had the throne on his mind.

Absalom bought a chariot, horses and bodyguards numbering fifty,

He got up every morning and went to the gate of the city.

People wanting to see the king coming from many different places,

Absalom said, "Being the judge, I would give justice to all cases."

When people tried to bow before him, he wouldn't take part,

Instead, he took their hands, kissed them and stole their hearts.

After forty years, he asked the king to go to Hebron to offer sacrifice,

He sent secret messengers to all tribes to rebel, preparing to fight.

Many others joined the conspiracy to take David off the throne,

David heard of the rebellion and quickly fled his home.

David had to move quickly, he knew it was a short time,

He and his entire household moved, only leaving ten concubines.

Once again, David is on the run,

From Saul to the Philistines and now his son.

Because Absalom couldn't see his father, he burned another man's field! Keep in mind he also murdered his brother, Amnon. Does this sound like a temper tantrum? All the while, David refused to discipline his son. Absalom had no fear of Joab, who is David's commander and a warrior. A spoiled rich kid that could do anything he wanted, and no one would say a word in fear of repercussions from daddy. So much so, he plotted to take over the throne.

2 Samuel chapter twelve speaks of David's own household rebelling against him and what will be done in the light. David's concubines play a part in this tale of David's downward spiral in 2 Samuel 16:20-22.

(2 Sam 14:25-33, 2 Sam 15:1-6, 2 Sam 15:7-17, 2 Sam 12:11-12, 2 Sam 16:20-22)

Hair at Two Hundred Shekels

David divided his army into a group of three,

Joab, Abishai, Ittai, and David will go out and lead the three.

The men said, "You will not go; you are worth more than our lives,

They won't care about us, even if half of us were to die."

Therefore, the king stood beside the gate as his army marched on,

David said, "For my sake, be gentle with the young man Absalom."

David's men met Israel in Ephraim's woods,

One army fell and one army stood.

The slaughter was great, 20,000 men laid down their lives,

More taken by the woods than the sword in the countryside.

Coming across David's men, Absalom tried to flee,

But as he rode, all his hair was caught in a tree.

One of David's men saw what happened and reported back,

"What?" Joab answered, "You saw him and didn't attack?

I would have rewarded you greatly."

The man said, "The king said to deal with him gently,

I wouldn't kill the king's son no matter the reward given to me,

The king would find out, and you yourself would abandon me."

Taking three darts, Joab plunged them into Absalom's heart,

In the killing of Absalom, ten of Joab's armor-bearers took part.

Joab blew the ram's horn and the men gave up the chase,

They threw Absalom's body in a deep pit and that was his fate.

Joab sent Cushi to David to bear the bad tides,

Ahimaaz also ran but not to tell Absalom lost his life.

And the king said unto Cushi, "Is the young man Absalom safe?"

Cushi said, "May those that rise against thee suffer the same fate."

I am curious to know, the verse saying, *more taken by the woods than the sword.* Do you think it was wild animals, snakes, or what do you think? Nonetheless, this is very important considering, 20,000 men lost their lives.

Absalom was praised in all of Israel for his beauty, from the sole of his foot to the crown of his head. His hair, which was only cut once a year because of the weight, weighed two hundred shekels. Converting shekel into pounds comes to about five pounds of hair. Is it any wonder why his hair was caught in the tree?

Joab, on the other hand, is still acting against the king's orders. He took it upon himself to kill the king's son and threw Absalom in a pit. Joab had no fear of the king. In 2 Samuel 19:4-7, Joab told the king what to do and if David didn't obey, he would face the consequences of disobedience. Eventually, Joab met his fate at the hands of Benaiah, Solomon's right hand.

(2 Sam 18:2-6, 1 Sam 18:4-13, 2 Sam 14:26, 2 Sam 18:14-17, 2 Sam 18:21-33, 2 Sam 14:25-26)

Counsel at Abel

The words of Sheba the Benjamite rang out,
He blew a trumpet, and these are the words he shouted.
"Down with David's dynasty,
We have no interest in the son of Jesse."
Therefore, all the men of Israel, they deserted him,
But Judah stayed with their king from Jordan to Jerusalem.
David arrived home and took the ten concubines he left,
Living in widowhood, they were shut up until the day of their death.
The king said to Amasa, "Assemble the men of Judah in three days,"
But Amasa tarried longer, not knowing this was his life's mistake.
David said to Abishai, "Sheba will do more harm if he escapes us,"
David didn't know Joab would render his own form of justice.
With all the warriors in pursuit, they met Amasa at the great stone,
Joab had a dagger poised to cut Amasa's flesh down to the bone.
He greeted Amasa by grabbing his beard with the right hand,
And smote him with the dagger in the left hand.
With Amasa's bowls spilled, there was no need to strike twice,
Amasa fell, and again, Joab took another innocent life.
Meanwhile, Sheba traveled all through the tribes until Abel's town,
Joab's forces in pursuit and eventually he was found.
All the people with Joab battered the wall, to throw it down,
"Here, here, say I pray you," came a woman's sound.
"Art thou Joab? Come hither that I might speak with thee,"
Joab came closer and said, "I am he."
She said, "Listen to what your servant has to say,
We are peaceful and faithful, why destroy us this day?
Long ago, they said, get your counsel at Abel, and that settled it,
Why do you want to swallow the Lord's inheritance?"
Joab said, "Hand over the man Sheba and we will withdraw,"
The woman said, "Behold, his head shall be thrown over the wall."
Going to the people with her advice and they cut off Sheba's head,
Threw it to Joab and they dispersed just as Joab had said.

Joab, again going against the king's orders, has killed another one of David's people. Do you think Joab murdered so many close to David to assure his place as commander of the army? People do a great many evils for power. Do you want power more than the blessings of the Father? Remember David's concubines Absalom slept with in 2 Samuel 16:22?

The woman that spoke with Joab must have been a respected elder in the town, because in this time, men generally were the ones who spoke up. She eventually went back to speak to the town and either informed them they would soon be under siege, or it is just best to cut off Sheba's head. Sometimes courage and wise words can prevent a disaster. Do you have the courage to speak up? Ask God for wisdom and the correct words before speaking, He will never let you down.

(2 Sam 20:1-10, 2 Sam 16:22, 2 Sam 20:15-18, 2 Sam 3:26-27, 2 Sam 20:21-26,)

There are more stories about David and his thirty mighty men. Please read about the heroics of the thirty and his battle with Goliath's family. Goliath's brother had a handle of a spear like a weaver's beam. Another giant had a total number of twenty-four fingers and toes. From 2 Samuel chapters 21 and 23 are stories about these men being loyal to David. Also 1 Chronicles 11:10-47.

Satan / Devil

Can we speak of God, without mentioning Satan? We cannot forget that Satan is an active participant in his attempt to lead you away from God, just as he did with the fallen angels. We need to stay in the word to be able to recognize when he comes, because he will, and he does. Keep your faith in God and keep praying for more and more strength. I know you have your bibles with you in a translation you understand, and you are reading four pages per day.

I'm Still Me

When I come, do you smell brimstone?

Do you see the mark of the beast on my dome?

But I'm called the Antichrist,

I'm the one that messed up your life.

I told you before that I'm bad to tha bone,

Keep reading and find out, I'm in that danger zone.

I'm still the Devil coming at you with my swag,

As they say, *poppa got a brand-new bag.*

Funny how God thinks you're a star,

Even when you don't know who you are.

With me, you keep trying to go round for round,

If not praying to God, you're not making a sound.

You lost the reason why you exist,

The love of the Father, you seem to miss.

Just one of the reasons you fail to rise,

It's so hard just to swallow your pride.

How about you not having any forgiveness,

Losing the reason on how Jesus lived.

The main reason why I'm the adversarial fight,

I can masquerade myself as an Angel of light.

Don't ask yourself why God created me,

That's just an excuse for why you don't believe.

I know He gave all you a choice,

And still, you listen to your own voice.

He gave you dominion,

But you listened to your own opinion.

This is when you forget to pray,

Or maybe you just lost faith.

Now, answer a question for me,

Do you like being deceived?

You are the one throwing away all of His words,

Me, I would rather reign in hell, than bow down and serve.

Because It's Fun

Why can't I stop sinning?

Because it's fun and I'm grinning.

The thrill of being caught,

Not caring about the lesson taught.

Now, the sin is easier the second time,

Now I have justifications in my mind.

I wouldn't do the things I do,

I flip it and put all the blame on you.

I wouldn't have done this,

If you stopped doing what I miss.

I tell myself, it's not really wrong,

Keep singing the same old song.

Giving credit, saying, I hear Satan's voice,

Knowing that I made a conscious choice.

If I don't seek the Father's word,

How do I know it was Satan's voice I heard?

No one sees me,

No one caught me.

I did it once and I can keep going,

Why stop, I can keep on sinning.

Counting backwards from ten to one,

Breaking them all because it's fun.

A Regular Day

Have I been busy questioning your Christianity?
Or perhaps questioning your humanity.
During the time of this pandemic,
Not knowing if you can stand this epidemic.
I see you still don't read all 66 books He gave you,
Like in Ecclesiastes 1:9, under the sun is nothing new.
People against people,
You know it's the same old evil.
I made this your focal point of concentration,
How about those still going through starvation?
I am so happy with your short memory,
Especially about the others still in need.
Homelessness and animal cruelty,
Lawlessness and child brutality.
Unemployment, the poor and the rich,
I'm laughing because you fall for the same tricks.
The minute my left hand is on the rise,
My right hand is plotting behind your eyes.
I know how short your attention span,
I knew this the day God created woman and man.
You blame each other,
You don't love your brother.
Money, power and greed,
That's all you need.
Then I throw a little something in the mix,
New generation, same ol tricks.
That's right I'm still the Devil,
I'm just taking it to a new level.
If you read God's words, you would know the signs,
Procrastinating, thinking you have more time.
The truth, the reality, so don't be dismayed,
For me, it's just a regular day.

26 and Counting

There are sixty-six in God's book,
Did you know, or did you have to look?
I have been called many names,
If you don't know them all, don't be ashamed.
I have been called a Lion and a Prince; twice,
An Anointed Cherub and an Angel of Light.
These names are so hideous,
Son of the Morning, now that's villainous.
I am going to give you this for free,
The scriptures that describe me.
In this poem, I will give only twenty-six,
However, if you know more, add them to the list.

Satan – Job 1:6, Now, there was a day when the sons of God came to present themselves before the Lord, and Satan came also among them.

Lucifer- Isaiah 14:12, How art thou fallen from heaven, O Lucifer, son of the morning! How art thou cut down to the ground, which didst weaken the nations!

Son of the morning- Isaiah 14:12, I got two names in this one.

Anointed Cherub- Ezekiel 28:14, Thou art the anointed cherub that covereth, and I have set thee so: thou wast upon the holy mountain of God; thou hast walked up and down in the midst of the stones of fire.

Devil- Matthew 4:1, Then was Jesus led up of the Spirit into the wilderness to be tempted of the devil.

Tempter- Matthew 4:3, And when the tempter came to him, he said, if thou be the Son of God, command that these stones be made of bread.

Prince of Devils- Matthew 9:34, But the Pharisees said, He casteth out the devils through the prince of the devils.

Beelzebub- Matthew 12:24, But when the Pharisees heard it, they said, this fellow doth not cast out devils, but by Beelzebub the prince of the devils.

The Wicked One- Matthew 13:19, When any one heareth the word of the Kingdom, and understandeth it not, then cometh the wicked one, and catcheth away that which was sown in his heart. This is he which received seed by the way side.

Enemy- Matthew 13:39, The enemy that sowed them is the devil; the harvest is the end of the world; and the reapers are the angels.

"I know, I racked up in the book of Matthew. Wait until you see the next three."

Liar- John 8:44, Ye are of your father the devil, and lusts of your father ye will do. He was a murderer for the beginning, and abode not in the truth, because there is no truth in him. When he speaketh a lie, he speaketh of his own: for he is a liar and the father of it.

Father of Lies- John 8:44

Murderer- John 8:44, as you can read, I got a three for one.

Prince of this World- John 14:30, Hereafter I will not talk much with you: for the prince of this world cometh, and hath nothing in me.

God of this World- 2 Corinthians 4:4, In whom the god of this world hath blinded the minds of them which believe not, lest the light of the glorious gospel of Christ, who is the image of God, should shine unto them.

Angel of Light- 2 Corinthians 11:14, And no marvel; for Satan himself transformed into an angel of light.

Belial- 2 Corinthians 6:15, And what concord hath Christ with Belial? Or what part hath he that believeth with an infidel?

Adversary- 1 Peter 5:8, Be sober, be vigilant; because your adversary the devil, as a roaring lion, walketh about, seeking whom he may devour.

Roaring lion- 1 Peter 5:8

Angel of bottomless pit- Revelation 9:11, And they had a king over them, which is the angel of the bottomless pit, whose name in the Hebrew tongue is Abaddon, but in the Greek tongue hath his name Apollyon.

Abaddon & Apollyon- Revelation 9:11

Dragon- Revelation 12:9, And the great dragon was cast out, that old serpent, called the Devil, and Satan, which deceiveth the whole world: he was cast out into the earth, and his angels were cast out with him.

Old Serpent- Revelation 12:9

Accuser of our Brethren- Revelation 12:10, And I heard a loud voice saying in heaven, now is come salvation, and strength, and the kingdom of our God, and the power of his Christ: for the accuser of our brethren is cast down, which accused them before our God day and night.

Now if you are counting, whether or not I placed twenty-six names,
Then you should be ashamed!
Because I keep score,
What is my name in John 8:44?
Yeah, I'm laughing,
What do you expect?
I'm the Devil.

1 Kings

I know you have your bible with you as we explore 1
Kings. This book of God's words speaks on David's
death, Solomon's reign, Elijah's ministry and
Rehoboam succession. David placed upon his
son Solomon to obey God's laws and to follow in
his ways. Solomon's only request was asking for
wisdom leading Israel. As Solomon's ascension
on the throne began with great success, the many
wives and concubines led him away from the
Heavenly Father.

Rehoboam also had the chance to lead in a just and
compassionate way but instead he listened to poor advice
leading to the division of the kingdom. Israel was split during the
rebellion with ten tribes led by Jeroboam and Judah and Benjamin
led by Rehoboam. With both tribes living in sin, God brought forth
one of the greatest prophets in Elijah.

I know you have your bibles with you in a translation you
understand. Please keep reading four pages per day and watch
how much you can accomplish and understand. God is amazing.

Monkey See

David is old and many blankets could not keep him warm,
They found a young virgin to look after him and keep him warm.
A girl by the name of Abishag, and brought her to the king for care,
She was beautiful but a romance, she and the king did not share.
Just as his brother Absalom, Adonijah wanted to rule,
The same as his brother, Adonijah was a fool.
Adonijah, whose mother was Haggith, began boasting,
Having chariots and runners he said, "I will make myself king."
He took Joab and Abiathar the priest to assist,
But Nathan, Benaiah and Zadok were left off the list.
He also invited all his brothers to the coronation,
Leaving out Solomon and the royal bodyguard from the celebration.
Nathan went to Bathsheba and said, "If you want to save your lives,
I suggest you listen to my advice.
Go to the king at once and ask about his promise,
Will Solomon be the next king on the throne he will sit?
You do not know Adonijah is calling himself king?
They sacrificed cattle and they are drinking and feasting."
Nathan said, "Has the king made a decision who will follow?"
"Thy son Solomon shall reign after me", David made the vow.
David ordered, "Place him on my mule and escort him back here,
Anoint him with oil and sound the horn for all the people to hear."
Zadok, Nathan and Benaiah took him to Gihon on David's mule,
When Adonijah found out what happened they felt like fools.
The people shouted with joy making such a sound,
The celebration was so joyous the noise shook the ground.
When Joab heard the horn,
They went into alarm.
Adonijah grabbed the horns of the altar, he was shaken to the bone,
Being summoned, Solomon dismissed him telling him to go home.

Adonijah was David's fourth son, and he did what Absalom did, which was rebel to take the throne. Parents know their children and Adonijah was not the son to sit on the throne. He lacked the leadership qualities it takes years to develop, which was a moral and spiritual character. David let his service to God neglect his service to his children. If this sounds familiar, remember Eli and his sons in 1 Samuel chapter 2. Can we be so heavenly minded that we are no earthly good? Bathsheba was the bridge between father and son. Nonetheless, Bathsheba was not without her faults. Adultery with David.

I am the youngest sibling, and I too mimicked my older brother trying to be like him. I also noticed the times he was placed on punishment for doing something he shouldn't have done. Those were the times I said to myself, that's not a good idea because of the penalties. Have you ever tried to emulate your older sibling? Or how about your parents or someone you admire? That can be a difficult task and an exhausting one trying to be someone you're not. We should strive to be the best you God has made.

(1 Kings 1:1-5, 1 Kings 1:11-16, 1 Kings 1:28-40, 1 Kings 1:49-52)

Cleaning House

David said, "Keep the charge of the Lord and do as he command,
Do this with all your heart and be a faithful man.
Obey this and one of your descendants will always sit on the throne."
David charged Solomon with this before God called him home.
David spoke of Joab, Barzillai and Shimei before he died in peace,
Advising Solomon actions as to not to appear weak.
One day Adonijah asked Bathsheba for Abishag the virgin,
He thought he could outsmart the wisest of men.
As promised, Bathsheba informed her son,
Solomon said, "You might as well give him the kingdom.
He's my older brother and he has Abiathar and Joab on his side,
He has proven not to be loyal and today he will die."
Benaiah carried out the act of execution,
Solomon relieved Abiathar the priest from his position.
Joab fled to the sacred tent thinking it was a safe place,
Refusing to come out, Joab sealed his own fate.
Benaiah informed Solomon and the king said, "Do as he said."
All but one of his enemies is now dead.
The king told Shimei to build a house but don't leave the city,
"On the day you cross the Kidron brook, I will have no pity"
Three years later Shimei broke his agreement,
Solomon must keep his word as one of David's descendants.
Benaiah took Shimei outside and killed him at Solomon's command,
Now, the kingdom was firmly in Solomon's hands.

David's advice was a reminder of the nagging thorns he never addressed. Joab spilled the innocent blood of Abner and Amasa. Shimei, who cursed him while he was fleeing from his son Absalom. Not all the advice was about taking out old thorns but also about the sons of Barzillai, who was very kind to him. I believe David's advice was not to extract vengeance but for people Solomon should keep an eye on who proved untrustworthy. We should always listen to great advice from people having our best interest in heart. Sometimes, I did not listen and did my *own* thing, which ended up in disaster. If I had listened to God or the people

God sent, the outcome would have been completely different. Do you listen, or decide you can handle situations your way?

Adonijah wanted Abishag for himself as a plot to take over the throne, but Solomon saw right through his scheme. The same as Absalom's rebellion in 2 Samuel 16:20-23, David saw his ulterior motives and eventually put a halt to them. During Solomon's time to clean house, Benaiah became the enforcer to carry out justice. He eventually became the commander of the army replacing Joab. Read about this fierce warrior in 2 Samuel 23:20-23, one of the *Thirty Mighty Men.*

(1 Kings 2:1-12, 1 Kings 2:13-26, 1 Kings 2:31-44)

Half-N-Half

The Lord asked, *"What do you want, ask and I will give it to you,"*
Solomon said, "You showed mercy to David for he walked in truth.
Your love has continued by allowing a son to sit on the throne today,
You made me a king, but I am like a child that doesn't know his way.
Give me an understanding heart to govern your people,
That I may know right or wrong and good or evil."
The Lord was pleased Solomon asked for wisdom,
And granted his request to wisely govern the kingdom.
"I will give you what you asked for,
But I will also give you more.
Riches and fame like no other king in the world of your life,
None will be compared to you and I will give you a long life.
Follow and obey my decrees as David did in the past,
I give you a wise and just heart such as no one will ever have."
Solomon awoke and he invited all his officials to a great feast,
In Jerusalem he sacrificed burnt offerings and offerings of peace.
Not long afterwards, came two harlots with a dispute,
Coming to the king not knowing what to do.
"We both lived in the same house and we both had babies,
Her baby died when she overlaid it and took mine from me.
She laid her dead son in my arms and took mine," one said,
"And the morning I went to nurse my son, he was dead.
In the morning light, I looked more closely,
And realized that this boy doesn't belong to me!"
The women in the presence of the king argued back and forth,
The king said, "You both claim the child, bring me a sword.
Cut the child the child in two and give each of them a half each,"
The mother cried out, "Give her the child, don't kill him please."
"All right, he will be neither mine nor thine," the other woman said,
Solomon said, "Give it to her that won't harm a hair on his head."
All of Israel was in awe of the king,
Seeing the wisdom and justice Solomon was rendering.

God asked Solomon what he wanted, and it would be granted, what a God. To Solomon's credit, he didn't ask for any material items or to live for an eternity, just wisdom. That is wisdom. Read what the bible says about wisdom in James 3:13-17. This brings us to the story of cutting a baby in half. Would you have thought of that? I believe any mother would not want to cause her child any harm but to think of that as a king and two women stating a claim, shows great wisdom. He did not use this wisdom all the time as king, look at 1 Kings 11:6-8. We should always keep in mind, if our wishes are granted; we should lean on the Lord obeying his guidance. Solomon was so wise; ambassadors from every nation came to listen to his wisdom, 1 Kings 4:34. However, he was not wise enough to avoid too many women leading him away from God.

(1 Kings 3:5-10, 1 Kings 3:11-15, 1 Kings 3:16-27, 2 Chron 1:7-10)

Too Much, Too Many

Solomon's wisdom and wealth grew as God decreed,

He built the temple and his palace no eyes could believe.

Building them both, it took a total of twenty years in all,

Now comes Solomon's greatness and the beginning of his downfall.

A visit from the queen of Sheba hearing of his fame,

All because he brought honor to the Lord's name.

She came with questions and she came with doubt,

She needed to see for herself what Solomon was all about.

She came with gold, jewels and many questions in her mind,

No question was too hard and no answer he could not find.

Sheba was overwhelmed and she exclaimed to the king,

"I didn't believe what was said but now I believe everything.

It is true, for I have seen it with my own eyes,

In fact, I have not heard half of it, you are very wise."

She gave about 1,000 pounds of gold, jewels and spices as gifts,

And cargoes of red sandalwood and more gold from Hiram's ships.

Each year, Solomon received many tons of gold,

All types of other riches and wealth untold.

Everything he had was made of gold, silver was considered worthless,

Every three years receiving gold and silver from Tharshish's ships.

Year after year, all brought him gifts and offerings,

Was this too much and did Solomon forget God's blessing?

Did Solomon have too much wealth? Did greed take over? How much is too much? Remember, you can't take it with you. When would you say, ok, that's enough? The Father did bless him with more than he asked but did it contribute to leading him away from God? How much wealth do you want? I think we all want to be comfortable but not having so much that it turns you from God.

Other royalty wanted to be close to Solomon based on his reputation. This is even true today. Do people latch onto a wealthy and or famous person just to be associated with them? There are others scheming with ulterior motives to do you harm when you are wealthy. As wise as Solomon was, could he not see some truths right under his nose?

(1 Kings 9:10, 1 Kings 10:1-10, 1 Kings 10:11-20, 1 Kings 10:23-29, 2 Chron 9:1-8)

Finding Time

Do not marry them because they will lead your heart away,

Yet, Solomon insisted on loving them anyway.

This was God's warning many years ago,

Solomon loved many foreign women, even the daughter of Pharaoh.

700 wives of royal birth and 300 concubines,

Did too many women make his faith blind?

He worshipped the goddess of the Zidonians and of the Ammonites,

In this way, Solomon did what was evil in the Lord's sight.

For all the foreign wives Solomon built them shrines,

Now the Lord had to speak with words divine.

"Since you have not kept my covenant and disobeyed my decrees,

I will surely rend the kingdom apart and take it away from thee.

But for the sake of David, I will not take the entire kingdom,

Because of my servant David, I will take it from your son.

All because you disobeyed and failed to follow my decree,

For my servant David and Jerusalem, my chosen city.

I will let him be king of one tribe,

Remember, this will happen when you die."

Are we as strong as we think? God knows our weaknesses and flaws. Pray for strength and wisdom when you feel weak. As wise as Solomon was, he was not wise enough to understand all his women would lead him away from God. Lust and desire. If this sounds familiar, remember Sampson lusted after Delilah, and how did that end? This is when temptation strikes, when you are vulnerable and at your lowest; you are not thinking straight. If the wisest of us all can fall to these temptations, why not you? Solomon is pulled in one thousand different directions, and he must have been mentally and physically exhausted. This is when we need God.

I believe this didn't happen overnight but a continual request to worship their gods. Have you ever given in to a spouse that constantly asks for something, and you gave in just because you grew weary of the request? Surrounded by sin spreading like an infectious disease going unchecked, Solomon yielded.

Remember, the sin we excuse is the deadliest because in our mind it is justified. Don't excuse it, confess it. Solomon's own words in Psalms 127:1 unless the Lord builds a house, the worth of the builders is wasted.

(1 Kings 11:1-4, 1 Kings 11:5-9, 1 Kings 11:10-13)

For David's Sake

As adversaries against Israel, the Lord rose up these men,
Hadad, Rezon and Jeroboam, marking the beginning of the end.
Hadad was royalty; he was of the king's seed,
Escaping from David as a boy to Egypt did he flee.
It came to pass in Edom, Joab and David, every male did they smite,
As a boy he escaped, now as a man, he is ready to fight.
While in Egypt, he found favor in Pharaoh's sight,
So much so, Pharaoh gave him land, a house and a wife.
When Hadad heard David and the captain of the host were dead,
He spoke to Pharaoh and this is what he said.
"Let me depart, that I may go to my own country,"
Pharaoh said," Is there anything you lack, or anything you need?"
Eventually, Pharaoh agreed,
This is the first of the adversarial seed.
Rezon son of Eliadah, God raised up as well,
Fleeing from his lord Hadadezer, he became leader of rebels.
After David conquered Hadadezer to Damascus did he flee,
He was an adversary to Solomon because he hated Israel intensely.
With adversaries from all sides,
This last one came from inside.
Jeroboam was industrious and placed in charge of the labor force,
This is the story of Jeroboam's rebellious course.
Jeroboam was leaving Jerusalem one day,
And met Ahijah the prophet along the way.
Ahijah took his garment and rent it into twelve pieces,
God saith, "*God will rend the kingdom and give ten tribes to thee.*
Solomon will have one tribe for my servant David's sake,
One tribe I have chosen from all others for Jerusalem's sake.
Because they have forsaken me,
Because Solomon has abandoned me.
Unlike his father David, Solomon has not done right in my eyes,
I will not take the entire kingdom, remaining a prince all his life.

My servant David, who kept my statutes and followed my commands,

I will take the kingdom from his son, placing ten tribes in your hands.

All that your soul desires, you shall rule,

Hearken unto all I command and here is what I will do.

I will give Israel unto thee,

A sure house I will build, just a David, because he obeyed me."

However, Solomon tried to kill Jeroboam but he fled,

Solomon sleeps with his fathers and Rehoboam rules in his stead.

Once you have read 1 Kings chapter eleven, you will read the number of times God said, for my servant David's sake. This exemplifies the respect God had for David because after all, he was a man after his own heart. God never breaks his promise. The same promise God gave to Solomon, but he let sin into his life and God tore the kingdom apart. I know you have your bibles with you, and you are reading four pages a day.

Solomon trying to kill Jeroboam sounds exactly like Saul attempts at David. Both had prophets informing them of the decisions of God and both becoming angry lashing out. Remember, who made the decision? God made the decision. Once again, we can't go against His decision or His promise. We need to stay out of the way, resulting in missing our own blessings.

(1 Kings 11:14-23, 1 Kings 11:23-25, 1 Kings 11:26-34, 1 Kings 11:35-42, 2 Sam 8:13-14)

Bones

Just as Jeroboam came to the altar to burn incense,
A man of God from Judah went to Bethel and said this.
"A child named Josiah will be born unto David's dynasty,
He shall offer priests and men's bones shall be burnt on thee.
This is the sign that the Lord has spoken,
Ashes on the altar will be poured out and the altar will be broken."
Jeroboam heard him speaking and said," Seize that man,"
Instantly, his hand dried up and he couldn't draw back his hand.
At the same time, the altar split, and the ashes poured,
"Please pray for me that my hand be restored."
Jeroboam said, "I will give you a gift if you come home with me."
The man said, "Giving me half of your house, I will not go with thee.
I will not eat or drink in this place, which is God's command,"
He left in a different way to leave Bethel's land.
As it happened, there was an old prophet still living,
His sons came home and spoke of the incident with the king.
He saddled his donkey and found the man of God under a tree,
Then he said, "Come to my home and break bread with me."
The man of god again repeated the Lord's command,
"I will neither eat bread nor drink water while in this land."
The old prophet lied and said, "An Angel came to me and spake,
Give him bread and water, to your house, you shall take."
The old prophet also said, "The Lord's command you disobeyed,
Because of this, your body shall not come unto thine father's grave."
The man of God finished, saddled his donkey, and started back,
Along the way, he was killed by a lion's attack.
Body in the road, people saw the donkey and lion standing by it,
The people went back to the town and reported it.
The lion did not attack the donkey, nor did it eat the man,
Showing the power of God for disobeying the Lord's command.
The old prophet in grief brought him home,
Telling his sons, "When I am dead, lay my bones beside his bones."

Jeroboam was going against a man God sent; of course, God would not allow anyone to attack His messenger. God punished him very lightly by drying up his hand, which could mean paralysis or a few medical issues. No matter the case, God's words are final. Like most, caught in the act, he tried to correct the mistake. Jeroboam tried but God had already given directions.

An older prophet also came to take the man of God off his assigned course, but this time he disobeyed God. When you receive direct communications from God, do you think He would send someone else to give a different message? Does God need a middle person? Perhaps we need to speak with God for clarity if we have any questions or confusion about His words. Do you think God will test us? Ask for guidance always, he will answer. God showed His power over the natural order of nature by stopping the lion to attack or eat the donkey or man. After all, God made everything.

(1 Kings 13:1-5, 1 Kings 13:11-20, 1 Kings 13:23-31,)

Masquerade

Jeroboam said to his wife, "Disguise thyself and get thee to Shiloh,

Speak to the prophet Ahijah about the child, he will know.

Take with you bread, cakes and honey as an offering,

He is the prophet that told me, I would be king."

The Lord told Ahijah, *"Not as herself, she will come to you,*

Listen carefully, I will tell you all you will need to do."

And it was so, when Ahijah heard the sound of her feet,

He said, "Come in, wife of Jeroboam, I have bad news for thee.

Tell Jeroboam the Lord says, *I exalted thee from among the people,*

You have not been like my servant David; you have done evil.

You have turned your back on me,

I will burn up your royal dynasty.

You have done more evil than all that lived before you,

Now, listen to what the Lord will do.

Every male from your house that dies in the city, dogs will eat,

And those males that dies in the field, the fowls will eat.

Go home, and when you enter the city, the child will die,

All of Israel will mourn; he is the only good in my eyes.

Even now, I will raise a king to rule; this happens today,

I will shake Israel like a reed because you have disobeyed.

He will root up Israel from this land,

And take it from Jeroboam's sinful hand."

How can you possibly think you can do evil, and God doesn't know about it? Does it matter if you are sending someone else to do your bidding? God still knows. When you are doing right by God, you can be blind, and God will take care of you. Ahijah knew who was coming long before they plotted their evil. Previously, God had dried up Jeroboam's hand and he didn't learn his lesson. How many times does it take us to learn our lesson once God gently punishes us? Hopefully, it will not take as many times as Jeroboam.

How many lessons are in this story? We can't fool God. We can't try to take advantage of the disabled. Don't send someone else to do our evil. There are consequences to our actions. Going against God pays a heavy price. I am sure you have some lessons of your own you have taken from this story. Keep reading and enjoying God's words.

(1 Kings 14:1-17, 1 Kings 16:1-4)

Faith's Power

Elijah told the king, "Until I give word, there will be no rain or dew,"

Then the Lord God told Elijah what to do.

"Hide by the brook Cherith by going east,

Drink from the brook and I commanded the ravens to feed thee."

And it came to pass, after a while; there was no rain in the land,

God said, *"Go to Zarephath, a widow will sustain you at my command."*

A woman gathering sticks as he arrived at the gates of the city,

"Fetch me; I pray thee, some water and food to eat."

She said, "As the Lord lives, I don't have any bread in my home,

I am gathering sticks, for me and my son are all alone.

After I prepare this last meal, we will die,"

Elijah said, "Fear not, ask and the Lord will provide.

Any of your barrels shall not come to an end,

Until the Lord God brings the rain, he'll send."

The widow did what Elijah asked,

The barrels never emptied as God's words came to pass.

Later, her son became ill and eventually took his last breath,

She said, "Have you come to me to cause my son's death?"

He took her son and carried him up to the room,

He cried out to God, "Why have you brought such doom?"

He laid the child on the bed and laid over him times three,

And said, "O Lord my God, let his soul come to him again please."

The Lord heard Elijah's voice and the child was revived,

Elijah took him to the widow and said, "See thy son is alive."

The beginning of Elijah's ministry, he was one of the greatest prophets in all of Israel history, if not the greatest. God shows His power by sending ravens to feed him day and night. Who else could do this? All His nature obeys Him, not Mother Nature but His nature Genesis 1:20-22. How many times has God used animals for His purpose? Think about these animals in different times in the bible, lion, donkey, serpent, and raven.

Elijah informed the widow, your barrels would never empty, until the rain comes again. Remember in 1 Kings 17:1, no rain for years and her barrels never emptied. What a God. Do we know when God will send someone for us to take care of? Will you? We should keep our ears, minds and hearts open to his voice. When He wants us, I think we will hear His voice.

Elijah, with God's power, brought the boy back from the dead. God is awesome. Keep reading the miracles through God, Elijah performs until God takes him in a whirlwind to heaven. His journey reveals the emotions he experienced of loneliness and despair in 1 Kings 19:3-4 and 19:10.

(1 Kings 17:1-6, 1 Kings 17:8-13, 1 Kings 17:14-17, 1 Kings 17:19-24)

Undefeated

The word of the Lord came to Elijah in the 3rd year,
"Go and show thyself unto Ahab, tell him the rain is near."
Meanwhile, the famine in Samaria became relentless,
King Ahab sent for Obadiah who oversaw his palace.
Now, Obadiah was steadfast to the Lord's will,
He hid 100 prophets that Jezebel tried to kill.
The king sent for him to help save his beasts,
Saying, "We must check everywhere to find grass for them to eat."
They each took a different way,
And Obadiah met Elijah along his way.
Obadiah said, "Is it you that draws near?"
Elijah said, "It is, go and tell thy lord, behold, Elijah is here."
Obadiah said, "How have I sinned, telling the king I will be slayed,"
Elijah said, "As the Lord lives, I will show myself this very day."
The king met Elijah and said, "Is it really you, you troublemaker?"
Elijah replied, "Only you and your family are the agitators.
You have refused to obey the Lord's will,
Now, summon all of Baal's prophets and all of Israel."
Elijah said, "How long will you waver between opinions of two,
If Baal is god, follow him, or follow the Lord that is true."
The people didn't make a sound,
Elijah spoke because he was honored bound.
"I am the only prophet left that has remained,
There are 450 prophets of Baal's domain.
Bring two bulls and the altar god sets fire for all to see,
Shall be the true God," and all the people agreed.
Baal's prophets went first, but it didn't set fire to the wood,
They called Baal's name, no answer as all the people stood.
Elijah began mocking them around noontime,
They shouted louder, cut themselves, but still Baal gave no sign.
Then Elijah called the people as he prepared the altar torn down,
He took 12 stones for the 12 tribes as the people gathered around.

He dug a trench and poured water all over the offering,

Now it was time for the sacrifice of the evening.

"Prove you are the God of Abraham, Isaac and Israel," Elijah prayed,

"O Lord, answer me and show all you are God this very day."

Instantly, fire of the Lord burned everything and the water around,

When the people saw it, they cried out and fell face down.

Elijah said, "Seize the prophets of Baal and don't let one escape.

He took them to the brook of Kishon and there they were slayed.

Even though Elijah was alone facing Jezebel and Ahab, he wasn't the only one being faithful to God. Obadiah hid 100 prophets in caves that remained true to God, which Elijah didn't know about. Just a reminder, you are never alone, you may not know about others, but God won't leave you alone. There are always others fighting the same fight but at different places and different ways.

Baal's prophets came in force and answered Elijah's challenge. He stood for God against many and remained confident God would prevail. After reading this, there are 850 prophets of Baal and the numerous worshippers surrounding him yet, God showed He was the one and true living God. So, I ask again, what can't God do?

We have read about the size of a problem with Goliath and now with the numbers that can be against you. Each time we read that only being faithful and truly open to His words, is the only way to His kingdom. How many times have you faced problems you didn't think you could overcome?

(1 Kings 18:1-6, 1 Kings 18:7-16, 1 King 18:18-24, 1 Kings 18:27-40, 1 Kings 16:30-33, 1King 16:31-33)

Behind Every Man

Close to the palace a vineyard Naboth owned,

Coveted by the king, he wanted to make it part of his throne.

The king spoke with Naboth and these are his words,

"Give me your vineyard that I may have it for a garden of herbs,

I will give you a better one or the price for it in money,"

Naboth said, "Lord forbid if I give my father's inheritance to thee."

King Ahab went home angry, and he refused to eat,

His wife Jezebel asked, "Why are you sad, what is wrong with thee."

He told her about Naboth's vineyard, he told her everything,

Jezebel said, "Is this how you act as being king?

Arise, eat bread and let thine heart be merry,

I will get Naboth's vineyard and give it to thee."

She wrote letters to the nobles and elders in Ahab's name,

In the letters, she wrote, and this is what she proclaimed.

"Proclaim a fast and set Naboth on high among the people,

And set two men, the sons of Belial before him to speak evil.

He spoke against God and the king, let them testify,

Then take him out and stone him so that he may die."

All did as Jezebel said,

Now Naboth is dead.

News reached Jezebel and she told the king to go and claim it,

Ahab rose up to go to the vineyard and took it.

And the word of the Lord came to Elijah,

"Arise, go meet Ahab, he is in Samaria.

Speak and say, you have murdered and stolen another man's property,

This is what the Lord shall do to thee.

Where the dogs licked Naboth's blood,

So shall the dogs lick up thine blood.

Behold, I will bring evil upon thee,

And I will take away thy prosperity.

You made Israel to sin, and you have angered me,

I will destroy all your male descendants either slave or free.

As far as Jezebel, the dogs shall eat her by Jezreel's wall,
Just as Baasha and Jeroboam, your house will fall."
Ahab heard the words and tore his clothes and went softly,
The Lord said, *"Do you see how he humbles himself before me?*
Because he has done this, I will not bring evil in his day,
However, I will bring evil upon his house in his son's day.

Have you ever met someone like Jezebel? She is cunning, ambitious, determined and a few more adjectives. Perhaps not to the point where they would kill someone but very focused on their goals of power. Jezebel ranks as the evilest woman in the Bible. The bible uses her name as an example of people who completely reject God in Revelation 2:20-21. Her end came by the hands of Jehu in 2 Kings 9:32-37.

(1 Kings 21:1-7, 1 Kings 21:8-14, 1 Kings 21:15-20, 1 Kings 21:23-29)

Inspirational 2

Let It Go

There are a few things we miss,

When it comes to forgiveness.

If you don't forgive others when they sin against you,

Your Father will not forgive yours in all that you do.

This is taken from Matthew 6:14-15, which is God's word,

But here are some more texts in case I'm not being heard.

Matthew 18:22 How many times shall I forgive, up to times seven?

Jesus says, "I tell you, not seven but until seventy times seven."

And we still haven't left the book of Matthew,

Are you starting to understand exactly what to do?

To have forgiveness is to have love,

The same love given to you by the Father above.

Luke 7:47, whoever has been forgiven less love less,

When are we going to stop the madness and end this mess?

Stuff that happened years ago,

Let it go.

The last time we spoke, I don't know,

Let it go.

We were young, now we're old folks,

Let it go.

I don't want to hear his name,

Just hearing it causes me pain.

We can't share the same space,

I don't want to see his face.

I want to be forgiven,

But I have anger for a foolish reason.

This is hurting my family,

And inside it is eating at me.

I love the cross from the bottom to the top,

But horizontally, I am still lost.

It seems as though you don't have enough texts,

So, listen closely to what is said next.

Job 7:21, why don't you forgive my offenses and my sins?
Listen to the next lines, it is important my friends.
We must forgive and release all of this inner torture,
Soon I will die, lie down in the dust, and I will be no more.
In other words, don't weep for me at my grave,
When I was alive is when you should have forgave.
These last lines, I will bring it home without any deception,
I'm writing this, looking at my own reflection.
Let it go.

My Aunt inspired this poem. My Aunt April Hardnett gave an incredible speech about forgiveness. Sometimes I hear speeches or sermons that seem as though the speaker is speaking to me directly; this was one of them. I am thankful for Aunt April and her words; this was a tearful and painful poem to write. I am sure I am not alone with forgiveness, but the good news is that the Father is always with us.

Sometimes, I have trouble forgiving others, especially when I can't understand the reason behind them hurting me in the first place. Meanwhile, the pain and hurt goes on for years without explanation or justification. My struggle is trying to understand the justification of not making any sense. I am not perfect, but I also know I am not where the Father wants me to be with forgiving others. I am not embarrassed or ashamed of my flaws, but I am working on it with the Father's help. I pray that He gives me strength in my struggles.

Careful

We should be careful when we pray,

God will give what you ask with the words you say.

We should come from a place of the spiritual heart,

Be careful, sometimes our heart is in a place that's dark.

Some may call it greed,

Asking for more than you need.

Trying to obtain more material wealth,

We forget about our spiritual health.

Always climbing the corporate chain,

We forget about our child's soccer game.

Or, it was someone's birthday,

Perhaps it's your anniversary day.

God gave you what you prayed for,

Just more, more and more.

The next time you are praying on your knees,

Start by having in your heart that you believe.

Believing in His power and His love,

The one true God above.

With a pure heart and pure mind,

Now He can bless you for all time.

You came with a conscience clear,

You came to Him being sincere.

Now God can give you what you say,

Just be humble to the Savior when you pray.

Grief

It hurts to see my friends grieve,

But we all grieve differently.

Some shut themselves in a dark room,

With no lights or sounds like a tomb.

Some lash out in an angry rage,

Not a second thought with the words they say.

Some need music in their ears and head,

Some curl up and don't leave the bed.

We all grieve differently,

Not all are the same, so let them be.

I handle my grief by what's in my heart,

The loss I feel rips me apart.

Let me grieve,

Let me be.

Don't criticize because I'm silent,

Even when my words can be violent.

Some act as if they don't care,

Some grieve in prayer.

We all have a different belief,

When we grieve.

Just pray to the Father to give you relief,

He will heal you and give you a new belief.

Youth

With so much sin surrounding our youth,

How do they get to Jesus to find all the truth?

When so many is fighting against them,

We need to rise and stand with them.

The world is fighting against the Kingdom they seek,

We must keep them on the path and Jesus they will reach.

Protect them,

Guide them,

Love them,

Cherish them,

Most of all pray for them.

We must do all we can to keep their innocence intact,

Shield them from all types of sinful attacks.

Keep them in the Father's house,

Let them know what Jesus is all about.

Keep them standing tall at the cross,

Let your spirit in and remove all doubt.

No doubt of your mercy and grace,

No doubt that your light shines on their face.

All our youth must do is to take a step towards you,

And watch how you will bless them with all that you do.

Jesus, keep them safe under your blessed wings,

Let them honor you when they lift their voice and sing.

Jesus our savior keep them protected,

Jesus our deliverer keep them uplifted.

Keep them Father and protect their life,

Keep them Father and bring them to Christ.

Struggle

As I'm falling deeper in sin,

This day I think the devil will win.

I have anger and I have rage,

No matter what is said, I still have hate.

Tonight, it seems like the darkness will come,

Only the Father can help me with His son.

I have tears because the darkness is getting stronger,

I don't know if I can hold out any longer.

I feel so desperate,

This life is a gift.

I am struggling through this night,

Hoping I will see God's light.

When we are in despair or darkness, only through prayer and faith can we stand tall for the Father. Asking for help is nothing to be ashamed of. God did not make only one person. We need others to pick us up when we fall. We should make a great effort to be of service to others and not seek anything in return. Allow yourself to be a blessing to others and let others bless you. Reach out to God, He will answer and get you through anything. God is awesome. Remember, there is nothing God cannot do.

In Need

Father help your son,
It's only you, yet no one.
I know you feel my pain,
I know you feel my strain.
Father, give me all I need,
Father help me to find peace.
Take my hand and guide me through the dark,
Touch my soul and place your spirit in my heart.
Hear my prayer,
Hear my despair.
Father hear my prayer,
Sweet Jesus hear my prayer.

A Different Mission

Christians,

Are we on a different mission?

Look in the mirror and what do you see?

All my sins looking back at me.

I'm not standing here being a self-righteous man,

If Jesus was here, He would write all my sins in the sand.

The same that call themselves God's people,

Are the same committing all types of evil.

There comes a time we must take a stand,

And not bury our heads in the sand.

Some that lead our congregations,

Cause so much negative devastation.

The same leaders posing as Christians,

Are the same leaders harming our children?

The same collecting our offerings and tithes,

Are the same living double lives.

But we're not supposed to see it,

And definitely not talk about it.

As Christians should we hide it?

Or should we take hold and get a grip on it?

How about the churches that have cliques?

Or the ones with pimps in the pulpit?

Or the ones with snakes in the sanctuary.

Is this the norm and should we worry?

As Christians what Bible do you read?

I thought Jesus said *all should come to me*!

If your health is bad,

If you're happy or mad,

Come to me.

If you're being abused,

If you're being used,

Come to me.

If you're a drug user,

If you're an alcoholic abuser,

Come to me.

Young or old,

I don't know what you've been told,

Come to me.

God's word says *come as you are*,

Jesus is the bright and morning star.

Christians,

Are we on a different mission?

Look in the mirror and what do you see?

All my sins looking back at me.

I'm not standing here being a self-righteous man,

If Jesus was here, He would write all my sins in the sand.

Do we have our brothers back?

Or are we slandering him with verbal attacks?

Are we happy when he does something positive in society?

Or are we bitter and mad showing negative jealousy?

Not the same congregation,

Not the same sexual orientation.

Not the same race or gender,

Not the same church or a member.

Not the same number of degrees,

Not the same college or university.

How many titles do you have?

You had a marriage that didn't last.

You had a child out of wedlock,

You listen to music that makes you drop it like it's hot.

You don't date those in your own church,

Does that mean they don't know the Lord's worth?

Should the question be what church do you attend?

After hearing the answer, the conversation comes to an end.

Should we push away?

Those wanting to be saved.

Those hungry for the word, close to Bible starvation,

Those that want faith and are ready for salvation.

Those going through adversities,

Those enduring all types of calamities.

Those knocking on Christ's door,

Then I ask what are we here for?

Just to say I have a position on the board,

Are you here for yourself or here for the Lord?

Are you here to take up all the spotlight?

Is it about you or is it about Christ?

Do we leave the church the same way we came in?

A forked tongue, troubled mind and hearts full of sin.

Christians,

Are we on a different mission?

Look in the mirror and what do you see?

All my sins looking back at me.

I'm not standing here being a self-righteous man,

If Jesus was here, He would write all my sins in the sand.

We are all guilty of casting stones,

We are all guilty of not taking care of our homes.

Are we Christians welcoming you with open arms?

Then later plotting to cause you harm.

From the first in line to the person at the end,

I think the word says a sin is a sin.

We need to remember walking in darkness is a choice,

We chose not to listen to Jesus and ignore His voice.

Can we all remember who is the boss?

And that there isn't a life outside the cross.

We must surrender to get restoration,

God almighty is our firm foundation.

Let each one – teach one,

In the name of the Father and Son.

I will do all with my God-given gifts,

I will tell all about the Holy Spirit.

I will let God's light shine,

All the way until the end of my time.

Christians,

We need to be on the same mission.

Look in the mirror and what do you see?

Living for Jesus by His grace and mercy.

I'm not standing here being a self-righteous man,

If Jesus was here, by me and for me He would stand.

Lil Man

Sometimes the jokes go over my head,

And I got a strange look about what was said.

My father gives that look that says tone it down,

The other men in the shop laugh and give each other a pound,

But I'm just happy to be hangin with pop,

I think I'm grown cause I'm down at the shop.

It's like grand central station,

Or the local place for men's vacation.

Some conversations are about life,

Some are about the problems with the wife.

Then there are some I'm not supposed to hear,

And my father says, "Just cover up your ears."

The man in the chair says, "Sorry lil man, I didn't know you were here,"

Pop looks at him that says watch your mouth, you know I'm sincere.

Now it's my turn to get my cut,

My feet don't move, I think I'm stuck.

The barber says, "Ok lil man, you're next,"

Pop just playfully slaps me on the back of my neck.

As the door opens, I hear the doorbell, cling, cling,

It's an announcement about who's arrived at the scene.

Someone is selling music and movies on DVDs',

Another is saying they got a trunk full of flat screen t.v.'s.

The barber asks, "Lil man what kind of cut?"

Pop tells him before my mouth opens up.

Now the sound of the clipper's motor roar in my ear,

I'm missing all the jokes I want to hear.

The clippers go off, barber says, "You owe me money,"

I'm thinking, how did it serious when all was joking and funny?

Barber says, "You lucky lil man is here or I'll tell you a few things,"

He gestures him to leave with a look saying you know what I mean.

Back to cutting saying, "Lil man I'm going to hook you up,"

I don't know what happened but I'm soaking it all up.

In my ears, it's the sound of the clippers moan,

And with my eyes seeing the fellas slapping bones.

It's like multiple movies playing at one time,

And I'm trying to sort it all out in my mind.

Pop is laughing,

Chest is out cause he's bragging.

Now everyone is looking at me,

I was so scared I almost peed.

Clippers off,

I gritted my teeth in my mouth.

All the men looking at me saying, "Keep it up lil man,"

Pop has my report card in his hand.

After a pat on the shoulder,

The barber has a mirror and says, "It's over."

The barber is done, and my cut is looking fresh,

Pop pays him and the barber says, "Who's next?"

We leave and pop says, "This is between us men,"

I say, "Yes sir," in my mind I can't wait til my hair grows again

Dedicated to my father Ervin Smith. He is missed, loved and with God. Remembering all the time, he took me to the barbershop for haircuts.

Love

If in heaven, do you think you could leave?

Well, Jesus did, even for those who do not believe.

Think about His sacrifice,

Coming to us leaving paradise.

Leaving the place as we know it, flowing with milk and honey,

No sin, no poverty, no hunger, and everyone is healthy.

If this is the season for giving, what did He give?

Only His life so that we all may live.

A place where there's not any pain, misery, or fears,

A place of joy, happiness and the absence of tears.

A place of peace, hope and love,

This is what He gave up, the one true God above.

Can anyone tell me that is not love?

But that is who He is and that is what He does.

God came here to show us He understands,

He showed us the path; He showed us the plan.

The plan of dedication,

The plan of salvation.

The plan of forgiveness,

The plan of Holiness.

The plan of everlasting life,

The plan of Heaven's high.

And because of God's plan,

We are washed by the blood of the lamb.

How can you not love your neighbor?

And expect to stay in God's favor.

How can you not love that child born in a manger?

That died on the cross we call our savior.

Because of His grace and mercy,

He died for you and He died for me.

With His dying breath,

He forgave us.

Forgive them Father; they know not what they do,
I love them Father as I also love you.
Even after, I was crucified on the cross,
My Father resurrected me, so all is not lost.
I know all the pain and temptation you go through,
When I come again, know that you don't have to.
Just keep believing in me my sons and daughters,
Remember that my Father had me walk on water.
He causes the deaf to hear and the blind to see with their own eyes,
He raised the dead from the tomb saying Lazarus come forth and rise.
He causes the poor to be rich and the weak to be strong,
Keep the faith my children my return won't be long.

Amen

Under God's Flag

And he sat upon the throne said, "Behold I make all things new,"

And he said unto me, "Write for the words are trustworthy and true.

I am coming soon, and my reward is with me,"

Those who are faithful will live an eternity.

One culture, one race, one love,

All united serving the one true God above.

You can listen to what you have been told,

You can travel the Earth and you can travel the globe.

Believing all these people can't be as one,

All of this diversity, all of them praising God's son.

Different cultures, different races,

Different genders, different faces.

Of all these languages we speak,

There is only one language we seek.

Those that keep His language shall be blessed,

Those that are faithful through temptations tests.

No matter the weapons formed, no matter the odds,

No matter how many differences, we are all standing for God.

Asking God for His mercy and His grace,

Praying to the Father to give us more faith.

Praying to the Father to change our hearts,

To give it more love before this world we depart.

Now we need to learn how to get along on this Earth,

We can't get to heaven without knowing forgiveness worth.

How can we pass through the pearly gates?

While on this Earth still having hate.

Do you want to walk on the golden streets?

And evil in your heart still has a beat.

But don't have any worries my family,

Jesus said all you have to do is believe in me.

None shall hunger and none shall thirst,

The first shall be last and last shall be first.

If you seek, he will find, if you ask it is given,

This is the promise from our Jesus who has risen.

He's the Alpha, the Omega the beginning and the end,

Do you want to be called when He comes again?

As all are standing and we are marching on,

Marching together to that beautiful city of Zion.

Love is Born

Wise men from all corners of the Earth,

Following the star pointing to Jesus' birth.

As shepherds watch from a Judean hill,

This is when God's love is fulfilled.

Starlight shining through all the darkness,

The great star for all the universe to witness.

Listen the trumpets are playing in your ear,

The Angel singing for all to hear.

Tonight, is the birth of the one,

Tonight, is the birth of God's son.

Love is born as the prince of peace,

Love is born God wants all to keep.

Love is born into our hearts,

A heavenly gift, a heavenly spark.

Love is born that we still have today,

A daily reminder, each time we kneel to pray.

Open your hearts and think of this,

God gave us His son as a heavenly gift.

Our savior was born in the middle of our sinfulness,

Given to this world to offer heavenly forgiveness.

The night Christ was born

2 Kings

Israel is divided between the kings of Israel and the kings
of Judah. Both kingdoms endured the succession
of evil rulers and eventually back into captivity.
Throughout this entire period, only two kings are
called good, Hezekiah and Josiah. These two did
what was good in the Lord's eyes all in the way
of David.

This book in the Bible also marks the death of
two of its greatest prophets, Elijah and Elisha.
You will read about the miracles performed through
their faithfulness to God. Elijah is nearing the end of his
ministry and Elisha is becoming God's voice in Israel.

This is the last book of the Bible for Poetic Scripture II, and I hope
you have enjoyed it as much as I enjoyed writing. I know you have
a Bible translation you enjoy reading and you are reading along
as you read my poetry. God is great and He wants to bless you
more than you can ever imagine. Keep the love for God and
each other near your hearts.

150

King Ahaziah fell through the lattice and became sick,

He sent messengers to inquire of Baalzebub to come back quick.

To ask god of Ekron about his recovery,

The Angel of the Lord told Elijah I am sending thee.

Say to them, "*It is because there is no God in Israel, that you inquire,*

Therefore, thou shall not come down from the bed; you will surely die"

The king asked, "Why have you returned so soon?"

The messengers told him a man giving a message of doom.

The king said, "What manner of man was he; what did he look like?"

"Hairy and girt with a girdle of leather on his waist" they replied.

The king already knew his name,

"Elijah the Tishbite!" the king exclaimed.

The king sent a captain and men numbering fifty,

The captain said, "Man of god the king said come down with me."

He said, "If I am, let fire from heaven consume thee and thy fifty,"

Then fire came from heaven and consumed the captain and his fifty.

The king sent another captain and another fifty men,

Fire came down and consumed this captain and his fifty again.

Then the king sent captain number three,

This time, the captain fell before Elijah on his knees.

"Spare our lives man of God I pray,"

And the Angel of the Lord said, "*Go with him, don't be afraid.*"

Elijah arose and went down with him to the king,

When Elijah arrived, he told him the same thing.

"You will die,

In the bed where you lie."

In my eyes, only the third captain had the sense to realize it is not a good idea to be against the man of God. It took 100 men to lose their lives before anyone understood God meant what he said. Reading carefully, the king knew about Elijah the Tishbite. Do we listen to the warnings God sends us? Or do we do our own thing? What are the results when we don't listen?

Remember, God can send anyone or anything. God can use his weather to send a message as a warning. Truly think about it. Have you ever thought that if you were at a place at a certain time, you would have been in a disaster? But, because of an unforeseen set of circumstances, you didn't make it? If you believe, it was a coincidence. Perhaps, but don't let it take 150 coincidences to realize God is with you.

Please read about Elijah being taken to heaven without ever tasting death 2 Kings 2:11. Elisha's first miracles 2 Kings 2:19-22.

(2 Kings 1:1-18)

As White as Snow

Naaman was the commander of king Aram's army,
Naaman, a mighty warrior, suffered from leprosy.
During battle, as captive they took a girl away,
She was given to Naaman's wife as a maid.
The girl said, "Going to the prophet in Samaria he will be healed,"
The king said, "Go, I will send a letter unto the king of Israel."
Naaman left with silver and gold,
And many sets of clothes.
The king of Israel read the letter and tore his clothes in dismay,
Saying, "Am I a god that I can give life and take it away?
I see that he is just trying to pick a fight with me,
Who am I to take away his leprosy?"
But when Elisha heard, he sent word to the king,
"Why did you tear your clothes, why do such a thing?
He will know there is a true prophet in Israel, send him to me,"
Naaman went to Elisha's house hoping to be cured of leprosy.
Elisha sent a messenger saying, "Wash in the Jordan seven times,"
Naaman said, "He didn't meet me," and thought Elisha was unkind.
Naaman officers said, "Go and wash yourself and be cured,"
Washing himself seven times, his skin became pure.
Naaman returned to the man of god with all his company,
Stood before him, thanked him and said, "Listen I pray thee,
I know that only in Israel there is a God in all the Earth,
Please take a blessing of thy servant of valuable worth."
"As surely as the Lord lives, I will not accept gifts," Elisha refused,
Naaman said, "Allow me to take earth from here on my mules.
From now on, only to the Lord will I offer sacrifices and offerings,
But may the Lord pardon me when I go to worship with the king.
In the house of Rimmon, when the king bows, he leans on me,"
Elisha said unto him, "Go in peace."
Gehazi, the servant of Elisha had evil in his heart,
Saying, "My master should accept gifts before the Syrians depart.

I will chase after him,

I will get something from him."

Seeing Gehazi coming, Naaman asked, "Is all well?"

Gehazi said, "My master sent me, behold what I tell.

Two men have come, he would like garments and a talent of silver,"

Naaman gave twice as much and sent two servants to deliver.

Gehazi didn't want Elisha to know he was being betrayed,

Before they reached the tower, Gehazi sent the servants on their way.

Elisha asked Gehazi, "Where have you been all this while?"

"I haven't been anywhere," Gehazi replied.

Elisha said, "Went not mine heart with thee?

When you chased down Naaman for money.

Is this the time for olive yards and garments to receive,

For cattle, servants, oxen, and sheep?

The leprosy of Naaman shall cleave unto thee,

Forever upon you and all of your seed."

During these times, leprosy was one of the most feared diseases of the land. We do not know what stage Naaman was in because he kept his position. He was a hero and humbling himself in a river and Elijah was beneath him. But is this not what God wants? Humbling yourself before Him. Remember, God's ways are best, and He can use whatever He wants to accomplish His purpose.

Gehazi saw a way to exploit money for God's favor, which was a mistake. Can you buy your way into heaven? Can you serve two masters Matthew 6:24? What did lies and deceit cost Gehazi? There is nothing evil about having money; only the way you use it and how it controls your life. True service is about love and devotion to God and seeks no personal gain. Love comes from the heart and who gave you a heart?

(2 Kings 5:1-7, 2 Kings 5:8-14, 2 Kings 5:15-19, 2 Kings 5:20-27)

Trampled

Benhadad mustered his Syrian army and Samaria was seized,

As a result, there was a great famine in the city.

For so long that a donkey's head sold for eighty pieces of silver,

The fourth part of a cab of dove's dung was five pieces of silver.

One day, the king was walking along the walls of the city,

A woman cried out, "My Lord the king, help me please."

A woman said to me today, "Let's eat your son,

And tomorrow we will eat my son.

So, we boiled my son, and he we did eat,

The next day, she hid her son so no eyes could see."

The king tore his clothes in despair, and this is what he said,

"God do so and more to me if Elisha's shoulders stay with his head."

Elisha was with the elders in his house when the messenger arrived,

Elisha knew the king was trying to take his life.

The messenger said, "This evil from God, for him why should I wait?"

Elisha replied, "Listen to the Lord, this is what he has to say,

A measure of flour will be one shekel and two measures of barley,

Behold, if the Lord makes windows in Heaven, might this be?

Thou shall see it,

But thou shall not eat it."

Now there were four men with leprosy,

They were at the gate entrance to the city.

They said, "If we go into the famine city, we will die,

Let's go to the Syrian's camp, hopefully they will spare our lives."

At dusk, they went to the camp but not a soul in sight,

The Lord caused them to hear a great army and they took flight.

The men with leprosy entered a tent and started eating and drinking,

They entered more tents and started plundering.

They took everything and hid it that no one could find,

But soon God's conscience entered their mind.

They said, "Mischief will befall us if we wait until morning,

Therefore come, that we may go tell the household of the king."

As the king got word, one of his officers thought it was a plot,

Saying, "They know we are hungry; they hid, and they will come out."

One servant said, "Of the five horses left, let's send one and see,"

And they went all the way to Jordan and returned to the city.

They reported back that not one Syrian soldier remained,

Then the people went out and plundered all that remained.

Just as the man of God foretold,

The price of flour and barley was sold.

As far as the man, that didn't believe,

He was trampled to death under the people's feet.

Let's start with God giving them a warning many years ago Deuteronomy 28:15-68. Even then, God spoke of the siege being so terrible that you will eat the flesh of your own children. How about the warnings the prophets said about having a human king instead of trusting God? Do you think the kings and the prophets were in constant conflict?

Now the lepers were a different part of the story that involves mercy. Remember lepers were not allowed into the city due to contagion. Again, God uses whom He wants. At first, they kept the good news to themselves, but God has a way to change their minds. They forgot about those starving inside the city. Is it any different about those who are starving for God's words? We need to spread the good news the same as the lepers and let all feast on the healing powers of God. We sometimes are caught up in our own mess that we forget to share the good news of Jesus.

(2 Kings 6:24-33, 2 Kings 7:1-6, 2 Kings 7:7-12, 2 Kings 7:13-20)

Who is with Me?

Elisha summoned a member of the prophets, "I have a task for you,
Take some olive oil; this is what the Lord wants you to do.
Find Jehu, speak to him, and from his friends take him away,
And this is what the Lord wants you to say.
Pour olive oil on his head and say *king, the Lord has made thee,*
Then open the door and flee."
The prophet went to Ramothgilead to complete his task,
He did everything as commanded that was asked.
He anointed Jehu and spoke for the Lord the words to tell,
"Smite Ahab and avenge the blood of my servants by the hands of Jezebel.
The whole house of Ahab shall perish entirely,
Like the house of Jeroboam and Baasha, destroy all of his family.
Jezebel, the dogs will eat, no one will bury her bones,"
The young prophet opened the door and fled home.
Jehu, against king Joram started a conspiracy,
He said, "Who is with me, let none escape the city."
The watchman shouted, "I see a company of troops coming,"
"Send a rider to ask if they come in peace," ordered the king.
The rider went out and asked, "The king asks if you come in peace?"
Jehu said, "What do you know about peace? Turn thee behind me."
The watchman said, "He has met them, but he is not coming back."
The king said, "Send another rider to find out if it is an attack."
The second rider went out and these are the words asked.
He rode to Jehu and asked, "Thus saith the king, is it peace?"
Jehu said, "What hast thou to do with peace, turn thee behind me."
The watchman said, "The driving is like Jehu; he drives furiously,"
And Joram said, "Get my chariot and make it battle ready."
King Joram and king Ahaziah met Jehu and asked, "Is it peace?"
Jehu said, "What peace, the witchcrafts of Jezebel are so many."
Joram yelled, "Treason" turned his chariot and started to depart,
Jehu with all his might shot an arrow and went out Joram's heart.
Jehu said to his officer, "Leave him in Naboth's land,"

They chased and killed Ahaziah, dying by Jehu's hand.

Hearing the news, Jezebel tired her head and painted her face,

Looking out a window saying, "Had Zimri peace in this place?"

Jehu looked up and shouted, "Who is on my side?"

Two or three eunuchs threw her out the window and she died.

Her blood went on the walls, horses, and he trode her under feet,

Jehu went into the palace and had a feast.

Jehu said, "Go and bury her, she was a king's daughter in this land,"

But they only found her skull, her feet, and palms of her hands.

As prophesied 1 Kings 19:16-17 Jehu was fulfilling God's promise. Also 2 Chronicles 22:7-9 all a part of God's plan. Ahab's evil dynasty had to be given justice as God foretold. Only lasting peace comes from God that gives it to us. Not only physical peace but also mental and spiritual peace. Do you have peace in your life?

Jezebel, all her power, wealth and luxuries made her think she can live forever. Death is the end, none of those items you can take with you. The time is now to set your life right with Christ, the end comes sooner than you think. Do you want His glory or yours?

(2 Kings 9:1-10, 2 Kings 9:14-22, 2 Kings 9:23-35)

Unfinished Business

The first letter to Samaria Jehu sent out,

Was for Ahab's sons to defend his house.

"Choose the worthiest of Ahab's seventy,

Place him on the throne and let him stand before me,"

The rulers and elders of Jezreel were exceedingly afraid,

They said, "Two kings stood not before him, how can we this day?"

Jehu's writing, "Tomorrow bring all the heads of your masters to me,"

They did, and the heads piled in two heaps at the gate of the city.

In the morning, Jehu went out to the people and said,

"I conspired, slayed my master but who took all these seventy heads?

Through Elijah God's message won't fail concerning Ahab's family"

Jehu slew all left of Ahab including officials, friends, and priests.

Jehu arose and came to Samaria at the shearing house in the way,

Another forty-two brethren of Ahaziah he had to slay.

When they arrived in Samaria, he killed the rest of Ahab's family,

But he had unfinished business, now it's time for all Baal's priests.

Jehu gathered all the people to hear him speak,

"Ahab served Baal a little, I will serve more, call for his priests.

Call everyone, for I am going to offer a great sacrifice,

Anyone who fails to come, make sure to take their life."

Jehu said, "Proclaim a solemn assembly throughout the land,"

Worshippers came to the house of Baal not leaving out one man.

Jehu made sure worshippers had a vestment on their back,

He also assured no one loyal to God was there before the attack.

Before Jehu went in to sacrifice, he had eighty men lay in wait,

He told them to slay them all and let none escape.

As soon as Jehu's offerings to Baal came to an end,

He gave the order to his men to let the slaughter begin.

None survived,

They paid with their lives.

They destroyed Baal's house,

Now it is a draught house.

All destroyed, except the calves of gold,

Now this is the message to Jehu from God is told.

Unto the house of Ahab, according to all that was in my heart

And until the fourth generation, the throne will not depart.

Jehu was ready to fulfill God's words, but he did go too far, Hosea 1:4-5. He was only to do what God instructed. Have you ever gone too far in the need to please God? Maybe not to the point of killing anyone but just did some extra instead of what God wanted. Jehu met Jehonadab son of Rechab and they rode to Samaria. Read what God says about the son of Rechab in Jeremiah 35 as an example to follow His words.

Why didn't Jehu destroy the golden calves? This is not the first-time golden calves are mentioned, Exodus 32:4. It is always easier to denounce the sins of others while excusing our own sins. In the end, God rewarded Jehu until the fourth generation. Only do exactly what God says or not. Either way, God will render His justice.

(2 Kings 10:1-8, 2 Kings 10:9-17, 2 Kings 10:18-23, 2 Kings 10:24-30)

Six Years Hidden

When Athaliah saw her son was dead,

She began to take all the royal family's heads.

Only one son of the king survived,

Jehosheba hid Joash and saved his life.

Joash and his nurse was hidden in the house of the Lord,

For six years, both of them weren't put to the sword.

In the seventh year Jehoiada sent word, all commanders come,

He made a pact with them and showed them the king's son.

He divided them up and put them into place,

One third will watch the house and another at Sur's gate.

"Ye shall keep guard of the Lord's house,

And ye shall compass the king roundabout.

All with weapons in hand,

Ready to slay any man."

To all the captains Jehoiada armed,

They stood from all corners of the temple arm-in-arm.

He brought forth the son and he was anointed king,

He was crowned, given the testimony, and the people were cheering.

When Athaliah saw this, "Treason, Treason," she cried,

She could not believe her eyes.

"Have her forth without ranges; all following kill with the sword",

The priests said," Let her not be slain in the house of the Lord."

She went by the way, by which the horses came,

And at that spot, she was slain.

Six years is a long time to hide a child and his nurse but during this time, the royal family was being beheaded. Hiding the King in the temple made sense, considering Athaliah, probably worshipped in pagan shrines, would have no interest in the Lord's temple. This shows the confusion with the bloodline and God's promise. God started to remove some of Israel's territory because of their rebellion to Him.

(2 Kings 9:27, 2 Kings 11:1-4, 2 Kings 11:5-11, 2 Kings 11:12-16, 2 Kings 10:32-33, 2 Chron 23:12-15)

Miracle After Death

Jehoash did what was right in the Lord's eyes,

All the days Jehoiada instructed him on what was right.

Yet he did not destroy the pagan shrines,

And the people still burned incense and offered sacrifices.

Until his last days when king Hazael on Jerusalem wanting to attack,

And his officers killed him plotting behind his back.

Now, Jehoahaz son of Jehu ruled over Israel's people,

But in the sight of the Lord, he did evil.

Because he followed the example of Jeroboam acts of sin,

In the battle against Hazael, they were defeated and couldn't win.

Because their oppression was so severe,

Jehoahaz prayed to the Lord hoping to reach His ear.

However, Israel did not depart from their sinful ways,

The Lord heard his prayer and sent a savior to save the day.

Not obeying the Lord, His words stand true,

Israel's army, once mighty, now stands only a few.

Jehoahaz died and his son Jehoash became king,

He ruled over Israel but only a few years numbering sixteen.

During this time, Elisha was close to his last breath,

King Jehoash visited him, he cried, and he wept.

Elisha said, "Put your hand on the bow,

And shoot out of the east window.

That arrow of the Lord will give you complete victory,

There is more to say, now listen to me.

Now take the other arrows and against the ground, strike,"

The king struck them three times with his might.

Angry, Elisha said, "You should have struck more times,

Now you will only beat Syria three times."

After speaking with the king, Elisha died,

Not the end of his miracles but the end of his life.

Later a band of Moabites invaded the land,

About this time, some Israelites were burying a man.

Spotting the raiders, they threw the corpse in Elisha's tomb hastily,
As the body touched Elisha's bones, he revived and stood on his feet.

God did promise Jehu his kingdom would last until the fourth generation 2 Kings 10:30. In 2 Kings 15:12 is the last of Jehu's generation sitting on the throne but only for six months. Jehoash did right in the Lord's eyes, but he did not destroy all the pagan shrines. When we aren't sure we have done all we can to correct our actions, we need to seek God for advice.

Joash only struck the arrows halfheartedly and not to the intent Elisha was trying to convey. If we don't follow God's instruction with our complete heart, why would you expect to receive His full blessings? How great was Elisha? How much did the Lord give him? Even in death, he blessed others and performed miracles. From chapters 14 to chapter 17 read about the many rulers and how they served or didn't serve the Lord. I know you have your favorite Bible with you as you read along. Remember four pages per day in a translation you enjoy.

(2 Kings 12:1-2, 2 Kings 12:17-20, 2 Kings 13:1-6, 2 Kings 13:14-21, 2 Kings 15:8-11)

The Threat

Now Hezekiah, son Ahaz had come,

He did what was pleasing, just as David had done.

He removed the high places, smashed stones and broke the poles,

Broke up the brazen serpent and cut down the groves.

He was successful in all he did, and God was by his side,

He revolted against Assyria, and this is the story of his life.

In the fourteenth year of his reign,

King Sennacherib of Assyria came.

And he took Judah's fenced cities,

Hezekiah said, "I have offended, I will pay monies."

To withdraw, this is the demand Hezekiah was told,

Three hundred talents of silver and thirty talents of gold.

Hezekiah gave him all the silver in the house of the Lord,

He stripped all the gold from the pillars and even the doors.

Nevertheless, Assyria sent a great army to confront the king,

It didn't matter about all the gold and silver he received as an offering.

There, Tartan, Rabsaris and Rabshakeh stood at Jerusalem doorway,

The king sent his officials to hear what they had to say.

Rabshakeh said, "Why are you confident to rebel against me?

Are you counting on Egypt that bends like a reed?

But if ye say unto me,

We trust the Lord our God; is not that he?

Hezekiah, himself tore down the high place,

It was Hezekiah that took them all away.

Pledge to my king and I will deliver 2000 horses to ride,

If you have enough men to ride them at your side.

Lord himself told us to attack you,

He told us to destroy you.

All of you listen to me,

You will eat your own dung and drink urine because you are thirsty."

Even in Hebrew, Rabshakeh shouted,

"Don't let Hezekiah fool you and come out.

The Lord won't save you,

The Lord won't rescue you.

Have any gods saved them from me?

Come out and everyone will eat of his own fig tree."

Everyone present and everyone heard,

Commanded by Hezekiah, no one said a word.

Hezekiah started a revival in the nation by destroying all the shrines and doing what was pleasing in the Lord's eyes. He broke the serpent pole of Moses called Nehushtan, which they started to idolize. Can we lose sight of a symbol of God and turn it into an idol? Remember, a symbol is only a symbol. Items only become a thing to worship by how we use them.

Assyria was a powerful nation and had already carried Israel away to Halah and to the cities of Medes in 2 Kings 17:6. What were they to fear? Judah, now a much smaller nation than before, starts to fall deeper into sin. Keep reading and find out how much the power of prayer and humbling yourself before God can achieve.

(2 Kings 18:1-6, 2 Kings 18:9-13, 2 Kings 18:14-19, 2 Kings 18:20-27, 2 Kings 18:28-36, 2 Chron 32:10-15)

I Got This

Hearing this, Hezekiah went to the house of the Lord,

Praying to God that his people wouldn't fall to the sword.

To Isaiah the prophet, Hezekiah officials came,

Informing Isaiah, the messenger of Assyria blasphemed God's name.

Isaiah said, "Don't fear any words coming from this man,

I will send a blast upon him; he will die by the sword in his land."

Assyria heard Ethiopia was attacking and they left,

But sent more messengers to Hezekiah to continue his threat.

And Hezekiah prayed before the Lord, "Bow down thine ear,

And oh Lord please hear.

Open Lord thine eyes,

It is you Assyria despise.

He has destroyed nations and their lands,

Gods made of wood and stone made by man's hands.

Father save us,

It is you we trust."

Then Isaiah sent this message to Hezekiah, these are his words,

"This is what the Lord God of Israel says, *I have heard.*

The virgin daughter of Zion hath despised thee,

The daughter of Jerusalem hath shaken her head at thee.

Whom has thou exalted thy voice and lifted thine eyes,

Even against the Holy One of Israel on Heavens high?

By messengers, you said you conquered mountains and cut down trees,

Dried up all the rivers with the sole of my feet.

But, have you not heard, I decided this long ago,

Now let me tell you what I know.

I know thy rage against me and I know thy abode,

I know every time you leave and everywhere you go.

I have heard your rage and how you blasphemed my name,

I will put my hook in your nose and send you back how you came.

Because you want to have a power grip,

I will also put my bridle in thine lips."

Then Isaiah said, "Here is the proof what God say is true,

A remnant of my people will spread out is what I shall do.

Concerning the king,

Don't worry about a thing.

He will not shoot an arrow, nor shall he cast a bank against it,

For I will defend this city to save it.

For my own sake,

And for my servant David's sake."

That night, an angel of the Lord 185,000 Assyrians soldiers killed,

Waking up the next morning to the corpses the land filled.

Then King Sennacherib broke camp and returned to his land,

Later his two sons smote him with swords in their hands.

I only have a few thoughts on this. When God says, *He got this* that should be enough. The statement in 2 Kings 19:34, *For I will defend this city, to save it, for mine own sake, and for my servant David's sake.* Wow. Please read what God informed Hezekiah about what He will do to Assyria in 2 Kings 19:22-33.

(2 Kings 19:1-7, 2 Kings 19:8-19, 2 Kings 19:20-25, 2 Kings 19:26-31, 2 kings 19:32-34, 2 Chron 32:20-21)

Figs and Ten Degrees

"Set your affairs in order, for you are going to die,"

This is the message Isaiah gave Hezekiah close to the end of his life.

When Hezekiah heard this, he turned his face to the wall and prayed,

"I have walked before in truth in all of my days."

While Hezekiah was weeping, Isaiah turned and left his side,

In the middle of the court God said," Turn *again I hear his cries.*

I will add fifteen years of life unto thee,

For my sake and for David's sake, I will deliver this city.

I will heal you, on the third day; you shall get out of bed,"

"Take a lump of figs and place it on the boil," Isaiah said.

Hezekiah said, "What will be the sign the Lord will heal me?"

Isaiah said, "Shall the shadow go forward or back ten degrees?"

Hezekiah said, "Make it go back because going forward is easy,"

Isaiah cried unto the Lord, and He brought it back ten degrees.

Berodachbaladan son of the king of Babylon sent letters and gifts,

Because he heard King Hezekiah had been very sick.

Receiving them, Hezekiah showed them all his precious things,

He showed them his entire house; he showed them everything.

Isaiah came, "Who are these men and what did they see?"

Hezekiah said, "Babylonians, they saw all including the treasury."

Isaiah said listen to God, "*The days come when all is taken away,*

All in thine house will be taken to Babylon, which thy fathers have laid.

Nothing shall be left,

Including thy sons, which thou shalt beget.

In the palace of Babylon, as eunuchs your sons will be,"

Hezekiah said, "Good is God's words, my days with truth and peace."

Hezekiah prayed and humbled himself before God and God heard his prayers. Do you think God hears your prayers when you come with an honest heart? Hezekiah was healed with figs placed on the boil. Do you think God gives doctors the knowledge today to heal the sick?

Were the Babylonian envoys a test to see what was really in Hezekiah's heart in 2 Chronicles 32:31? Did Hezekiah boast and brag about his wealth? Do you? God can take all that is given away. We should appreciate all that is given and learn to share the blessings we receive, not to boast about them. Give thanks for all God has given and take care of the things given.

(2 Kings 20:1-7, 2 Kings 20:8-10, 2 Kings 20:12-19, 2 Chron 32:24-26, 2 Chron 32:31)

Wiping Dishes

Manasseh for fifty-five years in Jerusalem did he reign,
He did what was evil not following the Lord's name.
He was only twelve years old when his reign began,
During most of his years, he was an evil man.
He built up the high places and set up pagan shrines,
He made his son pass through the fire and observed times.
He used enchantments, wizards and dealt with familiar spirits,
In the sight of the Lord, he wrought much wickedness.
He built altars in the Lord's house where God would put His name,
Manasseh provoked God to anger and brought much shame.
"My name will be forever in Jerusalem, my city,
The Lord told David and Solomon, *"If my people obey me.*
Observe the law my servant Moses gave my command,
Neither will I make the feet of Israel move from this land.
But they hearkened not and Manasseh seduced them,
Because he caused them to sin; now I will remove them."
God spoke through His prophets, *"He has done detestable things,*
More wicked than the Amorites, this is the disaster I will bring.
Both ears will tingle, whoever will hear of this,
I will wipe Jerusalem as a man wipeth a dish.
To their enemies, they will become prey,
Since their fathers came forth from Egypt, even until this day.
I have been provoked to anger because of the evil against my will,
Moreover, Manasseh shed innocent blood until Jerusalem was filled.
He caused Judah to sin and didn't do what was right,
Always leading them to do evil in the Lord's sight."

It says much when you provoke God to anger, considering He is slow to anger in Exodus 34:6.
How angry do you think God was? He did say both ears will tingle when anyone hears about
what He does to Jerusalem. Can you imagine the sin that Manasseh did to cause this anger?

However, in 2 Chronicles 33:10-13, Manasseh is humbled by God and is taken away to Babylon. In prison, he prayed for forgiveness, God heard his prayers, and he was brought back to Jerusalem to do God's will. If God can forgive Manasseh, surely, He can forgive us. Remember, to come with an honest heart and be humble. Are you heavy hearted with guilt that no one can forgive you? Please remember, no one is beyond the reach of the Father's forgiveness.

(2 Kings 21:1-5, 2 Kings 21:6-10, 2 King 21:11-16, 2 Chron 33:10-13)

Unquenchable

Josiah was eight years old when he became king,

He followed the examples of David, in the Lord's eye was pleasing.

During the restoration of the Lord's temple, they found a book,

It was the book of the law and Josiah was shook.

The words of the laws were read to the king by the priest,

Josiah listened and tore his clothes in grief.

He said, "Inquire for us God's words, His wrath is great,"

And to the house of the Lord to the prophetess did they take,

Huldah said, *"The Lord says I will bring evil upon the city,*

All have worshipped other gods and have forsaken me.

They have provoked me to anger with the works of their hands,

You have burned incense to other gods from foreign lands.

My wrath shall be kindled against this place, and it shall not be quenched,

Now go to the King of Judah who sent you and tell him this.

I have heard thee,

You have humbled before me.

Because thine heart was tender and true,

Behold, this is what I will do.

I will bring this evil, but you will not see it with thine own eyes,

All of this will happen after you die."

I know you have your favorite bible with you. How many times have the Lord informed someone when you pray with an honest heart and come to me humbly, I forgive you? Sounds like a reoccurring theme and excellent advice. We need to understand not to repeat the same sins but to pray for strength.

Josiah was eight when he began to reign. No one is too young to start obeying God's words. No matter the age, God uses whom He wants. Do you think you are too old or young to be used by God? Your work for God can begin today, just ask.

What do you think the book of the law was? The Law of Moses? Whatever it was, they took it to a prophetess. How many prophetess were there up to this point? I can count a few, Miriam Exodus 15:20 and Deborah Judges 4:4. Again, God can use whom He wants no matter the age or gender. What a God we serve.

(2 Kings 22:1-7, 2 Kings 22:8-11, 2 Kings 22:12-20, 2 Chron 34:22-28, 2 Chron 35:22-24)

Babylonians

Josiah has died and he was buried in the land,
Now comes the evil, just as the Lord's command.
And Nebuchadnezzar from Babylon to Jerusalem's city,
He took all the wealth and put King Jehoiachin into captivity.
Nebuchadnezzar king of Babylon came with his host, one and all,
Built forts, pitched against it, with the act that Jerusalem will fall.
The city was broken, and the men fled by night,
The king went the way toward the plain, fleeing Babylon's might.
His army scattered and on the plains of Jericho, they caught him,
And at Riblah, the king of Babylon passed judgment on him.
They gouged out eyes and in fetter of brass carried him to Babylon,
Moreover, right before his eyes, they slaughtered all his sons.
Now Nebuzaradan captain of Babylon's guard arrived,
He burned the house of the Lord with the Chaldees army at his side.
The captain of the guard took all the fugitives he could find,
He didn't take them all; he left the poor of the land behind.
All the brass and gold were taken away,
It was so much; they did not know the weight.
He took the gatekeepers and all the priests,
Even all the officers that were found in the city.
Back to Riblah, all the people he did take,
And all of them the king of Babylon slayed.
In the land of Judah, all the people that remained,
He placed them under Gedaliah's reign.
When the captains of the armies heard about this,
They went to him and gave him a well wish.
Now from the royal seed, Ishmael son of Nethaniah came,
And with ten men, Gedaliah and the Jews were slain.
All of those remaining, to Egypt they wanted to disappear,
The captains of the army both small and great were in fear.
Later, Jehoiachin, king of Judah that was in captivity,
Was set free by Evilmerodach of Babylon and shown pity.

All of this happened at the Lord's command because the people were led into sin. Do you think the leaders that led people to sin will pay a higher price? What about our leaders today? We hear about leaders stealing, raping, and committing other sins, what will be their price to pay? The Babylonians only did what God had planned to do to His people that had forsaken Him. The Babylonians invaded Judah three times, giving His people time to repent 2 Kings 24:1, 24:10 and 25:1.

(2 Kings 23:29-30, 2 Kings 24:10-16, 2 Kings 25:1-7, 2 Kings 25:9-17, 2 Kings 25:18-21, 2 Kings 25:22-26, 2 Kings 25:27-30, 2 Chron 36:17-20)

This was the last book of the bible in Poetic Scripture II. I hope you enjoyed reading the poetry as much as I enjoyed writing. Please continue to read God's words and become one with Him. He loves us. Love your neighbor as you love yourself. Love and forgiveness, always. Reading and writing gives me the opportunity to open myself to His love and the love of others. I know I fall short of His glory but through prayer, I am walking towards Him. I thank you for taking your time to take this poetic journey with me. God bless.

Ladies Chapter

In the chapter, Ladies chapter is a special dedication to my extraordinary wife, Melody Smith, and my amazing mother Yvonne M. Smith. It is also honoring all the strong women I have had the pleasure of meeting, past, present, and future.

The next three poems are a story of the bond between mother and daughter. Only they can truly understand this heavenly bond. I hope I have done justice in my attempt to capture the story in poetry. This is a girl's journey to womanhood and the love they share ending in motherhood and celebration.

Above Queen

She teaches me that all should have respect,

And that I should love myself without regret.

Sometimes we go shopping just mother and daughter,

And she teaches me about the love I have from my father.

She teaches me the right way to be a little lady,

All without neglecting myself or losing my identity.

It is part of the heavenly bond we share,

While telling me stories when brushing my hair.

The joy of the first time we baked my favorite cookies,

Or remembering the time she called me her mini me.

All the times she wiped my tears away,

Giving me advice with the words she would say.

Raise your words, not your voice,

You are a lady and you have a choice.

Face challenges with confidence,

And ask God to give you patience.

Don't' forget to help someone along the way,

And ask God for guidance so you won't be betrayed.

Please remember to ask God for His wisdom,

This is for your journey for things to come.

Jesus will hold me up when I can't stand,

On her knees, mom prays for His plan.

The plan to keep me safe,

The plan to live in His grace.

Mom gave me this and many more things,

Mom is a title, just above Queen.

Strength Within

Mom cried when I left to go to college,

And said, "This is half, the rest is God's knowledge."

I told her not to cry because of how you raised me,

You taught me to trust God and it is Him I believe.

Mom, I remember the time we picked out my prom dress,

And you said, "I know he's your date but don't take no mess."

I remember when I graduated with my degree,

You were so proud and said, "You're still my mini me."

I'm a full-grown lady now but still daddy's little girl,

I know at all costs; he would still give me the world.

From the time, I thought my first job would be so hard,

Now with God's blessings, I'm the supervisor in charge.

Mom, I thank you for helping me plan my wedding,

You and dad accepted my husband and that was a blessing.

No matter what was going on in my life,

You are the rock guiding me to do what's right.

You have been not only my mom but also a good friend,

When we hang out together, people say we look like twins.

From the time you gave me life and to this very day,

Our bond is strong because to the Father we both pray.

Mom, you have given me the blueprint on what a mom should be,

I am telling you this because of the life growing inside me.

I will still need your prayers, patience and guidance,

Don't worry, since a young girl, you gave me confidence.

And I will teach her the great values you imprinted in me,

The love of family and always pray to God on your knees.

Your strength within guided me through all my days,

Mom, I love you now and always.

Legacy

A child's laughter through the kitchen's window is the sound we share,

We both have a silent smile as I gently brush my mom's hair.

She starts telling stories about what I did when I was a kid,

Then says, "You are the reason why I live.

But child, let me tell you, you were a handful,

And your father stopped me twice because I lost my cool.

I remember you came home looking like a hot mess,

Stood in the doorway looking pitiful because you tore your dress.

And I told your father, *that is your child*!

Went upstairs because I had to pray awhile."

"I know mom, mines just did that to me,"

Mom laughed and said, "The apple is not too far from the tree."

I gently tugged her hair,

We make such a pair.

My daughter runs in and says, "I love you," then back out the door,

Mom holds my hand and says, "I know that's what you live for."

My husband comes in and firmly gives me a kiss,

Out the door so our daughter has someone to play with.

Granddad saying, "I better help; she'll run him in the ground,"

We both give him that look without making a sound.

Then huge laughter as he looks back,

Mom gets up and starts making snacks.

We hear laughter, giggles and "Mom, daddy tickling me!"

I whisper saying, "My daddy did the same to me."

Mom didn't say a word,

I don't know if she heard.

But tears drop from her eyes,

I understand why she cries.

We go to the window hand in hand,

Two people as one when we stand.

I turn to her and softly say,

"This is the reason why we pray.

This is your granddaughter, a part of us, a part of we,

This is part of your bloodline and a part of your legacy."

Melody

What are the words and tunes to my Melody?

My heart sings to her because she is part of me.

Like a pianist, you play the keys to my heart,

Continue playing the notes and we will never be apart.

The honeymoon song is coming to an end,

Now let the songs of our love start to begin.

I know the love we have is not wrong,

Because I hear the notes of my Melody's song.

Just keep loving me for being me,

One day you will have me on bended knee.

I love making you smile and want you to be mine,

I want this feeling to last all our lifetime.

This is our very first birthday,

Only a few words I need to say.

On this day, God created you,

Just know that I love you.

Your muse

Quiet Storm

This was one of the first poems I wrote for Melody. Since then, she has become my wife, my love and my Melody in my heart. I love you.

Love Letter

To my beautiful wife: Melody

You are my love and my life. You have been my rock and my conscience from the beginning. You have kept me grounded when I thought I could fly, but still let me spread my wings. I thank you for allowing me to be me. You are an amazing woman. You have my heart and make me want to write more poetry to my Melody. As I am writing this love letter to you, I am crying tears of joy with the love we have. I pray everyone can be as blessed as I am. You love the Lord and seek Him first, that melts my heart. You are the song and Melody in my heart. I love you now and always. I love our saying, *A happy us there is no fuss.*

Quiet Storm

Rhythm with Melody

What is good music without a Melody?

How can you dance without a good beat?

There is only one chorus in this song,

A steady beat lasting a lifetime long.

The rhythm is in tune to the beat of my heart,

And it is erratic and slow when we're apart.

How we sway back and forth as if in a trance,

Holding each other as one in our special dance.

Snare drums, keyboard, guitar and bell,

I'm so in love with you, can't you tell?

Trumpet, saxophone or any instrument of choice,

No matter how many are playing, I only hear your voice.

I only hear your rhythm and Melody,

Only because you are part of me.

Respect

Mother's Day from one year to the next,

There are many words to describe it, but I call it respect.

Respect for all the years,

Respect for all the tears.

Respect for all the nights I caused you grief,

Respect for the hours you prayed on your knees.

During adolescence when I thought, I was the man,

And you lived by the fair and firm hand.

All the times you worried for me late at night,

The rules I didn't understand and wanted to fight.

Now I know the rules kept me out of jail,

Now I know your house wasn't put up for bail.

I know about the two rules of the street,

Prison or the grave is where I could be.

I understand why you have prayed,

I have more respect for Mother's Day.

All the days you had me study the school's lesson plan,

Understanding you wanted me to be a better man.

All the times you pushed me to go to college,

No matter how old you get, you can still get knowledge.

Whether it's your job or if it's in your life,

School is always in session even if you don't try.

Sometimes it comes when you least expect it,

But listen, you can still learn so respect it.

Even if you think, it's coming from an old fool,

Yes, they too can take you to school.

I understand why you have prayed,

I have more respect for Mother's Day.

Respect for keeping shelter over my head,

And a place to lie when I go to bed.

Respect for the meals cooked when I needed to eat,

Thank you for the clothes on my back and shoes on my feet.

Respect for going to work and getting your work grind on,
Being exhausted but still having time to spend with your son.
Respect for taking me to church,
And teaching me about self-worth.
Respect for teaching me God's plan will never fail,
And don't chase money because it's not the Holy Grail.
Respect for teaching me to appreciate what I have,
Because if you don't honor God, it will not last.
I truly understand why you pray,
I have respect now and more respect every day.
Happy Mother's Day.

Just One

Dear Father, I have a question about one and no other,

How is she, how is my mother?

I know you have her,

But I miss her.

She taught me about you,

That your words are sacred and true.

You recently called her home,

You called her to be by your side at your throne.

These are the days I miss her advice,

Staying on the phone late in the night.

I miss her laughter,

I miss her character.

Without her, at times, I feel afraid,

Other times, I feel I won't make it through the day.

Sometimes I feel the armies of darkness closing in,

Sometimes I feel like they will win.

I miss my mother I miss my friend,

I wish I could speak to her again.

Father, I am here with tears in my eyes,

And all I can ask is why?

My son, if she taught you about me,

Then you should know we both are with thee.

The days you are lost and afraid,

She sends an Angel to point the way.

When you think you won't make it through the day,

Just fall to your knees and start to pray.

I will make sure she hears your words,

I will make sure all your words are heard.

Don't let the sorrow into your heart,

Remember your bond and the joy will never depart.

Yes, I called my daughter home,

Yet, you are never alone.

Yes, the enemy is closing in, but it is not a defeat,
They want to attack you, thinking you're weak.
Just like Elijah, keep faith and I will open your eyes,
I will send heaven's army to stand by your side.
I called your mother to end her pain,
We both knew you would never be the same.
She knows about the man she raised,
She knows you will be faithful until your last day.
Until the day I call you home,
Until the day you will come sit by my throne.
Remember, I sacrificed my son for you,
Remain faithful and remain true.
Keep my son Christ with all things that you do,
And when I whisper your name, your mother is here waiting for you.

In loving memory of Yvonne M. Smith. You are missed and loved so much. No words can express the love I have for my mother and all the lessons she taught. The only way I can see her again is to obey God and pray He has a place for me at His table. I love you mom.

Day

I love my mother
Today is my Mother's Day
So is everyday

Defend

A son's love for mom
Who dares to stand in between?
Standing to defend

Unconditionally

From the start of life
Mom protects you from danger
Until eyes are closed

Nature/Nurture

Is it nature or?
Is it nurture their children?
I think it is both

Mom

Always love your mom
Enjoy all the time you have
You only get one

Wife

Melody is love
My heart sings with happiness
Her name brings me joy

Sis

My sisters are great
Friends until the very end
They are cool like that

Behold

Looking as a man
The love of mom and daughter
A joy to behold

Bond

How tight is their bond?
Mother and daughter are one
Nothing can divide

Serve

This is my princess
Mom is a step above queen
We serve each other

Dedicated to my father and mother, Ervin and Yvonne
Smith. They are missed and loved always.

Printed in the United States
by Baker & Taylor Publisher Services